NEW TOPICS FOR SECONDARY SCHOOL MATHEMATICS
Materials and Software

MATRICES

Department of Mathematics and Computer Science
North Carolina School of Science and Mathematics

NATIONAL COUNCIL OF TEACHERS OF MATHEMATICS

Copyright © 1988 by
THE NATIONAL COUNCIL OF TEACHERS OF MATHEMATICS, INC.
1906 Association Drive, Reston, Virginia 22091
All rights reserved

Second printing 1991

Library of Congress Cataloging-in-Publication Data:

(Revised for vol. [3])

New topics for secondary school mathematics.

   Contents: [1] Geometric probability—[2] Data
analysis—[3] Matrices.
   1. Mathematics—1961–   I. North Carolina
School of Science and Mathematics. Dept. of Mathematics
and Computer Science.
QA37.2.N49 1988   510   88-5305
ISBN 0-87353-258-9 (set)
ISBN 0-87353-270-8

Printed in the United States of America

Contents

Preface

These materials on matrices are drawn from a course developed by the Department of Mathematics and Computer Science at the North Carolina School of Science and Mathematics. This course, developed under funding from the Carnegie Corporation of New York, is called *Introduction to College Mathematics* (ICM) and is designed to prepare high school students who have completed Algebra 2 for the variety of mathematics they will encounter in college and beyond.

The content and focus of the ICM course respond to recommendations on secondary mathematics made by the College Board, the National Council of Teachers of Mathematics, the Sloan Foundation, and the National Science Foundation. The course provides a foundation to support future coursework in mathematics including calculus, finite mathematics, discrete mathematics, statistics, and mathematical modeling. Furthermore, the course provides an introduction to the mathematics used in engineering, the physical sciences, the life sciences, business, finance, and computer science. A primary goal of ICM is to immerse students in applications-oriented, investigative mathematics so that students will better understand the technological world in which they live. The problem-solving experiences in the course require students to synthesize skills and content. Real-world applications are used to motivate students to study some traditional precalculus topics; however, the course goes beyond the traditional precalculus curriculum to provide students with mathematical experiences that will prepare them for future courses and careers. These experiences include analysis of data, an introduction to algorithms, work with discrete phenomena, and exposure to mathematical modeling. The course integrates extensive use of calculators and computers. In addition, many sections of the ICM materials are designed with the assumption that a microcomputer is available to use for demonstrations and investigations in front of the classroom.

The content goals of the *Matrices* unit are to use matrices to model real-world phenomena, to use matrices as discrete data structures, and to understand the elementary matrix algebra needed in various mathematical models. Matrices may be familiar to many students; however, matrix algebra is often taught in secondary schools with little motivation in the form of realistic applications. The focus of this unit is <u>not</u> on using matrices to solve problems students can handle without matrices, such as the methods of determinants and matrices for solving systems of linear equations. Rather, this unit presents matrices in contexts that empower students to solve problems that would be considerably more difficult, or not feasible at all, without the use of matrices. The materials in this unit can be judged a success if, by studying this unit, students would begin to understand the power that mathematical structures such as matrices can offer for problem solving and applications.

Although the *Matrices* unit was written as part of the ICM course, the content is well suited to stand alone or to be incorporated into other courses. Most sections require only the skills usually mastered in Algebra I. However, section 7, Computer Graphics, also requires some knowledge of trigonometry.

The first three sections—"Introduction and Overview","Matrix Addition and Scalar Multiplication", and "A Common-Sense Approach to Matrix Multiplication"—should be presented in the order given in the text. After the first three sections, any or all of the remaining sections can be completed. Furthermore, sections 4 through 7 are independent of one another, so they can be presented in any order.

Section 4, "The Leontief Input-Output Model and the Inverse of a Matrix," presents the work of Nobel laureate Wassily Leontief as motivation for learning a method of finding the inverse of a matrix. The method of elementary row operations is presented as a method for inverting matrices. Using these mathematical techniques, Leontief's model is applied to some simplified economies.

Section 5, "The Leslie Matrix Model," provides a matrix model for age-specific population growth. The distribution of a population by age is modeled using the Leslie matrix and matrix multiplication. A subsection on stabilizing population growth through harvesting or reduction of birth rates is included at the end of this section, although its mastery should not be considered essential for all students.

Section 6, "Markov Chains," uses matrix multiplication in modeling the long-term probabilities of various outcomes associated with certain phenomena. Although the concept of probability is treated quite informally, some extra background in probability may be helpful for students.

Section 7, "Computer Graphics," presents matrix methods used to implement graphics with computer software. This section is more abstract and results-oriented than the other sections. Students who enjoy computer programming will find that this section offers a number of interesting and challenging programming projects.

Numerous examples and exercises are included in each section. Examples in the text are highlighted by introductory titles and concluding box symbols (■). "Class Practice" exercises are designed to be integrated into classroom discussions or completed while a student works through the materials. "Exercises" are provided for student assignments. Answers to all exercises are given in the section entitled "Answers to Exercises."

Computer software and a user's guide accompany this unit. The software provides the tools for performing all of the matrix calculations found in this unit. Some sections can be covered without using the software; however, Sections 5 and 6 require the use of the computer to generate matrices raised to large powers. Some of the options provided by the software include defining static, dynamic, identity, and constant matrices with up to 15 rows and 15 columns; viewing and printing already defined matrices; performing matrix calculations including matrix addition, scalar multiplication, matrix multiplication, raising matrices to powers, and finding the inverses of matrices; and performing the elementary row operations used for inverting a matrix. If possible, the software should be used with all sections of this unit. It will eliminate the drudgery of massive calculations and enable the student to focus on understanding the concepts associated with the matrix models.

Matrices

1 Introduction and Overview

Three major countries that produce cars for sale in the U.S. are Japan, Germany, and the U.S. itself. When it is time to buy a new car, people will choose a car based in part on the satisfaction they have received from the car they presently own. Suppose that of car buyers who presently own a U.S. car, 55% will purchase another American-made car, 25% will buy a Japanese-made car, 10% will buy a German-made car, and 10% will buy a car made in none of these three countries. Of those who presently own a Japanese car, 60% will buy another Japanese car, whereas 25% will buy American, 10% German, and 5% none of the three. Of those car buyers who own a German car, 40% will again purchase a German car, 35% will switch to American cars, 15% will switch to Japanese cars, and 10% will buy from another country. Of those who presently own a car from a country other than the three major producers, 20% will switch to American, 25% will switch to Japanese, 15% will switch to German, and 40% will continue to buy from another country.

The details of this information are difficult to grasp all at once; however, the following display of the data offers distinct advantages over the verbal description given above.

$$
T = \begin{array}{c} \\ U.S. \\ Jap. \\ Ger. \\ Other \end{array}
\begin{array}{cccc} U.S. & Jap. & Ger. & Other \\ \left(\begin{array}{cccc} 0.55 & 0.25 & 0.10 & 0.10 \\ 0.25 & 0.60 & 0.10 & 0.05 \\ 0.35 & 0.15 & 0.40 & 0.10 \\ 0.20 & 0.25 & 0.15 & 0.40 \end{array} \right) \end{array}
$$

The table of numbers T shown above is an example of a *matrix*, in which the numbers are known as *entries*. The *dimension* of a matrix is given by the number of rows and number of columns, so that T is considered a 4×4 matrix. If a matrix has m rows and n columns, then it is said to be an $m \times n$ matrix. If $m = n$, as in T, then the matrix is called *square*. Individual entries in a matrix are identified by row number and column number, in that order. For example, the number 0.05 is the entry in row 2 and column 4 of T, abbreviated as T_{24}. We also have $T_{32} = 0.15$ and $T_{13} = 0.10$ as two other entries in the matrix T.

Each entry in T has a specific, unique meaning; therefore, the dimension of a matrix cannot be reduced without losing essential information. In T, the rows represent the country of origin of the presently owned car, whereas the columns represent the origin of the next car. T is an example of a *transition matrix*, for it contains information concerning the owner's transition from the present car to the new car. The concept of a transition matrix is essential to the later section on Markov chains.

When mathematics is used to analyze real-world phenomena, the interaction of mathematical concepts and the real world is often based upon data. We apply mathematics to information that

1

is gathered through measurement and observation. The discipline of mathematics includes many concepts that aid us in analyzing and interpreting data, so that data can be used and expressed in summary form. Various data representations exist that allow us to discern trends, to form generalizations, and to make predictions, all on the basis of data. For example, an economist may use a linear function to forecast the growth of an industry. A biologist may use an exponential function to predict when the world population will exceed 10 billion. These two examples are characterized by using mathematics to describe the behavior of a given situation, a process called *mathematical modeling*. Most of the mathematical models studied in school involve real-world phenomena approximated by continuous functions, which have graphs that can be drawn without lifting the pencil from the paper, such as lines and parabolas. A principal advantage of using continuous functions is the availability of a large body of well-developed theoretical results, such as those studied in high school algebra and precalculus courses.

A matrix, on the other hand, is used with a collection of data that does not lend itself to the use of a continuous model. *Matrices* (the plural of matrix) are part of a larger branch of mathematics called *discrete mathematics*. The term discrete refers to the fact that these techniques of mathematical modeling deal with finite sets of noncontinuous data rather than continuous functions or continuous sets of data. The advantage of using a matrix to organize a set of data is illustrated by the preceding example of purchasing cars. Just as a functional rule like $f(x) = x^2$ is a good continuous model for certain real-world phenomena (the trajectory of a falling object, for example), a matrix is a mathematical tool used to handle noncontinuous data sets in summary form. Because matrices operate with discrete data, they possess dimension; that is, a matrix cannot be reduced to a single number such as the value of a function at a point. A matrix can be thought of as a single entity for the sake of simplicity; however, it is a single entity that contains many data values. In addition, just as special algebraic rules exist for functions, matrices have a special algebra associated with them. Although matrix algebra seems rather peculiar at first, it involves operations defined in ways that allow matrices to be used in many mathematical models. As a complement to the repertoire of continuous techniques emphasized in secondary school mathematics, the following sections introduce methods for using matrices to model discrete data.

2 Matrix Addition and Scalar Multiplication

We begin this section with a problem that illustrates the operations of matrix addition and scalar multiplication.

Example 1—The Hobby-Shop Problem: Suppose that you have a small woodworking shop in your garage and you make toys for children as a hobby. Lately you have begun selling your toys at the local flea market. You make four different kinds of toys, namely a train (t), an airplane (a), a dragon (d), and a nameplate (n). Each of these can be made very plainly out of pine (p), or with greater detail and ornamentation out of oak (o). Let matrices O, N, and D represent your sales for October, November, and December, as given below.

$$O = \begin{matrix} \\ p \\ o \end{matrix} \begin{pmatrix} t & a & d & n \\ 3 & 5 & 0 & 2 \\ 1 & 2 & 1 & 3 \end{pmatrix} \qquad N = \begin{matrix} \\ p \\ o \end{matrix} \begin{pmatrix} t & a & d & n \\ 4 & 2 & 1 & 3 \\ 1 & 0 & 2 & 4 \end{pmatrix} \qquad D = \begin{matrix} \\ p \\ o \end{matrix} \begin{pmatrix} t & a & d & n \\ 4 & 8 & 5 & 3 \\ 4 & 2 & 1 & 6 \end{pmatrix}$$

Notice that, as with the transition matrix of the previous example, each entry in matrices O, N, and D has a specific meaning. For example, the number of pine dragons made in December is given by entry D_{13}, which is 5. How many oak trains were made in November? What does O_{24} represent?

We will now examine the following question: how many of each item were sold for the entire three month period?

The total number of pine trains sold is $3 + 4 + 4 = 11$, which is the sum of the numbers in the upper-left corner of each matrix. The total number of oak dragons is $1 + 2 + 1 = 4$, which is the sum of the entries in row 2 and column 3, or

$$O_{23} + N_{23} + D_{23} = 4.$$

We can construct a matrix S that has entries representing the total number of each item sold during the three months. From the pattern established above, we see that each entry of S is the sum of the corresponding entries of O, N, and D. In symbols, we have

$$S_{ij} = O_{ij} + N_{ij} + D_{ij},$$

and S contains the entries shown below:

$$S = \begin{array}{c} \\ p \\ o \end{array} \begin{pmatrix} t & a & d & n \\ 11 & 15 & 6 & 8 \\ 6 & 4 & 4 & 13 \end{pmatrix}$$

The fact that each entry of S equals the sum of the corresponding entries in O, N, and D is represented by the matrix sum

$$S = O + N + D.$$

Addition of matrices is a common-sense operation. Since each entry in a matrix represents a category by its position in the matrix, the operation of matrix addition is performed by adding the corresponding entries in each matrix. Adding matrices provides a concise structure for organizing an otherwise complicated operation. For example, in the Hobby-Shop Problem, the single matrix sum $S = O + N + D$ represents 8 sums of 3 numbers each.

Example 2: Using the data from Example 1, suppose that in the following year you sell the same number of each item in October, double the number sold of each item in November, and triple the number sold in December. How many of each item do you sell during the three months?

The matrices O', N', and D' that we want to add are shown below:

$$O' = \begin{array}{c} \\ p \\ o \end{array} \begin{pmatrix} t & a & d & n \\ 3 & 5 & 0 & 2 \\ 1 & 2 & 1 & 3 \end{pmatrix} \quad N' = \begin{array}{c} \\ p \\ o \end{array} \begin{pmatrix} t & a & d & n \\ 8 & 4 & 2 & 6 \\ 2 & 0 & 4 & 8 \end{pmatrix} \quad D' = \begin{array}{c} \\ p \\ o \end{array} \begin{pmatrix} t & a & d & n \\ 12 & 24 & 15 & 9 \\ 12 & 6 & 3 & 18 \end{pmatrix}$$

The entries of O' are identical to O. Each entry of N' is twice the corresponding entry of N, which we can represent by the notation

$$N' = 2N.$$

The number 2, which is not a matrix, is a dimensionless quantity called a *scalar*. The result of a matrix multiplied by a scalar, called *scalar multiplication*, is a matrix derived by multiplying each entry of the original matrix by the scalar. Thus, we also have

$$D' = 3D.$$

Using scalar multiplication, we can represent S', the number sold during the three months, by

$$S' = O' + N' + D',$$

or, equivalently,

$$S' = O + 2N + 3D,$$

which gives

$$S' = \begin{array}{c} \\ p \\ o \end{array} \begin{pmatrix} t & a & d & n \\ 23 & 33 & 17 & 17 \\ 15 & 8 & 8 & 29 \end{pmatrix}.$$

■

Matrix addition and scalar multiplication have reasonable definitions; likewise, subtraction of matrices is defined just as you would expect—finding the difference of corresponding entries.

Example 3: Suppose that in the original Hobby-Shop Problem, we know that sales for the entire year are given by the matrix Y below:

$$Y = \begin{array}{c} \\ p \\ o \end{array} \begin{pmatrix} t & a & d & n \\ 26 & 25 & 14 & 16 \\ 13 & 7 & 8 & 28 \end{pmatrix}$$

How many of each item did you sell during the months other than October, November, and December? The answer is given by the matrix R defined as

$$\begin{aligned} R &= Y - (O + N + D) \\ &= Y - S. \end{aligned}$$

The result is

$$R = \begin{array}{c} \\ p \\ o \end{array} \begin{pmatrix} t & a & d & n \\ 15 & 10 & 8 & 8 \\ 7 & 3 & 4 & 15 \end{pmatrix}.$$

■

Addition and subtraction of matrices require that the matrices be of the same dimension, meaning that they must have the same number of rows and the same number of columns. Furthermore, the corresponding rows and columns must have identical interpretations. Each row and column of a matrix has a specific meaning; therefore, trying to add or subtract matrices with different row or column labels is an attempt to combine incompatible quantities.

2.1 Exercises

1. The Campus Bookstore's inventory of books consists of the following quantities:

    Hardcover: textbooks—5280; fiction—1680; nonfiction—2320; reference—1890.
    Paperback: textbooks—1940; fiction—2810; nonfiction—1490; reference—2070.

    The College Bookstore's inventory of books consists of the following quantities:

    Hardcover: textbooks—6340; fiction—2220; nonfiction—1790; reference—1980.
    Paperback: textbooks—2050; fiction—3100; nonfiction—1720; reference—2710.

    (a) Represent the inventory of the Campus Bookstore as a matrix.
    (b) Represent the inventory of the College Bookstore as a matrix.
    (c) Use matrix algebra to determine the total inventory of a new company formed by the merger of the College Bookstore and the Campus Bookstore.

2. The Lucrative Bank has three branches in Durham: Northgate (N), Downtown (D), and South Square (S). Matrix A shows the number of accounts of each type—checking (c), savings (s), and market (m)—at each branch office on January 1.

$$A = \begin{array}{c} N \\ D \\ S \end{array} \begin{pmatrix} c & s & m \\ 40039 & 10135 & 512 \\ 15231 & 8751 & 105 \\ 25612 & 12187 & 97 \end{pmatrix}$$

    Matrix B shows the number of accounts of each type at each branch that were opened during the first quarter, and matrix C shows the number of accounts closed during the first quarter.

$$B = \begin{array}{c} N \\ D \\ S \end{array} \begin{pmatrix} c & s & m \\ 5209 & 2506 & 48 \\ 1224 & 405 & 17 \\ 2055 & 771 & 21 \end{pmatrix} \qquad C = \begin{array}{c} N \\ D \\ S \end{array} \begin{pmatrix} c & s & m \\ 2780 & 1100 & 32 \\ 565 & 189 & 25 \\ 824 & 235 & 14 \end{pmatrix}$$

    (a) Calculate the matrix representing the number of accounts of each type at each location at the end of the first quarter.
    (b) The sudden closing of a large textile plant has led bank analysts to estimate that all accounts will decline in number by 7% during the second quarter. Calculate a matrix that represents the anticipated number of each type of account at each branch at the end of the second quarter. Assume that fractions of accounts are rounded to integer values.
    (c) The bank president announces that the Lucrative Bank will merge with the Me. D. Okra Bank, which has branches in the same locations as those of the Lucrative Bank. The accounts at each branch of the Me. D. Okra Bank on January 1 are:

$$\begin{array}{c} N \\ D \\ S \end{array} \begin{pmatrix} c & s & m \\ 1345 & 2531 & 52 \\ 783 & 1987 & 137 \\ 2106 & 3765 & 813 \end{pmatrix}$$

Find the total number of accounts of each type at each branch of the bank formed by the merger of the two banks. Use the January 1 figures and assume that the accounts stay at their current branch offices.

3   A Common-Sense Approach to Matrix Multiplication

In the previous section, we saw that matrices can be used to organize information that is otherwise more difficult to grasp. We also saw that matrix addition and scalar multiplication are defined just as one would expect, given the meaning attached to the data in a matrix. Is it likewise possible to define matrix multiplication in a common-sense way that relates to real-life situations? The multiplication of integers can be thought of as repeated additions. For example, 5 times 3 can be thought of as $5 + 5 + 5$. This interpretation can be applied to scalar multiplication, since $3A$ is equal to the sum $A + A + A$. The product AB of two matrices A and B does not fit the same interpretation: A cannot be added to itself B times, since B is a matrix, not a number. The following example provides a consistent interpretation for matrix multiplication.

Example 1—The Cutting-Board Problem: You and a friend decide to go into a partnership making cutting boards and selling them at the local flea market. Suppose that each of you makes 3 different types of cutting boards:

- Style 1: made of alternating oak and walnut strips

- Style 2: made of oak, walnut, and cherry strips

- Style 3: made in a checkerboard pattern of walnut and cherry

You and your partner plan to make the number of cutting boards of each style shown in matrix A.

$$A = \begin{array}{c} \\ You \\ Part \end{array} \begin{pmatrix} 1 & 2 & 3 \\ 8 & 4 & 6 \\ 6 & 6 & 8 \end{pmatrix}$$

Each cutting board is made by gluing together one-inch strips of wood of the appropriate type in the desired pattern. Matrix B describes the number of strips of oak (o), walnut (w), and cherry (c) needed for each style.

$$B = \begin{array}{c} 1 \\ 2 \\ 3 \end{array} \begin{pmatrix} o & w & c \\ 10 & 10 & 0 \\ 8 & 6 & 6 \\ 0 & 10 & 10 \end{pmatrix}$$

To determine how much of each type of wood you need to allocate to produce the cutting boards listed in matrix A, we will examine the following questions.

(a) How much oak will you use to make the cutting boards?

You will make 8 boards of Style 1, each of which uses 10 oak strips; 4 boards of Style 2, each of which uses 8 oak strips; and 6 boards of Style 3, which uses no oak. The total number of oak strips you will use is expressed by the sum of the products

$$8(10) + 4(8) + 6(0) = 112,$$

so you need a total of 112 oak strips.

(b) **How much oak will your partner use?**

Your partner will use an amount of oak given by the sum

$$6(10) + 6(8) + 8(0) = 108,$$

so your partner requires a total of 108 oak strips.

(c) **How much cherry will you use?**

The amount of cherry you will use is

$$8(0) + 4(6) + 6(10) = 84$$

for a total of 84 cherry strips.

∎

For each of the questions above, we found the amount of a particular type of wood you or your partner need through addition of the products obtained from multiplying the number to be made of each style by the corresponding amount of the wood needed to make one cutting board. In each sum, the first factors are numbers from a row of A, whereas the second factors are from a column of B. We can summarize the amount of wood you and your partner will use with the following matrix C, in which the entries are the numbers of wood strips:

$$C = \begin{array}{c} \\ You \\ Part \end{array} \begin{array}{ccc} o & w & c \\ \begin{pmatrix} 112 & 164 & 84 \\ 108 & 176 & 116 \end{pmatrix} \end{array}$$

Observe that the entry in the first row and first column of C is obtained by lining up the first row of A and the first column of B, then multiplying the corresponding entries and adding the products together. Row 1 of A and column 1 of B are

$$You \begin{array}{ccc} 1 & 2 & 3 \\ \begin{pmatrix} 8 & 4 & 6 \end{pmatrix} \end{array} \quad \begin{array}{c} \\ 1 \\ 2 \\ 3 \end{array} \begin{array}{c} o \\ \begin{pmatrix} 10 \\ 8 \\ 0 \end{pmatrix} \end{array}.$$

Multiplying pairwise term by term gives

$$8(10) + 4(8) + 6(0) = 112;$$

this sum is entry C_{11}. Likewise, entry C_{23} is obtained by multiplying pairwise term by term the second row of A by the third column of B, as shown below.

$$Part \begin{pmatrix} 1 & 2 & 3 \\ 6 & 6 & 8 \end{pmatrix} \begin{matrix} 1 \\ 2 \\ 3 \end{matrix}\begin{pmatrix} c \\ 0 \\ 6 \\ 10 \end{pmatrix} = 6(0) + 6(6) + 8(10)$$

$$= 116$$

What row of A multiplied by what column of B gives entry C_{12}? The entry in the first row and second column of C is found by multiplying the first row of A by the second column of B.

All of the entries in C can be found using the method illustrated above. This way of combining entries in two matrices to yield a third matrix is called *matrix multiplication*; matrix C is defined as the product of matrices A and B. The operation can be written in the form shown below.

$$C = AB$$

$$= \begin{matrix} You \\ Part \end{matrix}\begin{pmatrix} 1 & 2 & 3 \\ 8 & 4 & 6 \\ 6 & 6 & 8 \end{pmatrix} \begin{matrix} 1 \\ 2 \\ 3 \end{matrix}\begin{pmatrix} o & w & c \\ 10 & 10 & 0 \\ 8 & 6 & 6 \\ 0 & 10 & 10 \end{pmatrix}$$

$$= \begin{matrix} You \\ Part \end{matrix}\begin{pmatrix} o & w & c \\ 112 & 164 & 84 \\ 108 & 176 & 116 \end{pmatrix}$$

In general, the matrix multiplication $C = AB$ is defined as follows: Each entry C_{ij} is obtained by multiplying pairwise term by term the ith row of the first matrix A by the jth column of the second matrix B. In symbols, this definition means that

$$C_{ij} = A_{i1}B_{1j} + A_{i2}B_{2j} + A_{i3}B_{3j} + \cdots + A_{in}B_{nj}.$$

Example 2: Let matrix D represent the cost in dollars per strip for each type of wood in the Cutting-Board Problem.

$$D = \begin{matrix} o \\ w \\ c \end{matrix}\begin{pmatrix} Cost \\ 0.18 \\ 0.22 \\ 0.20 \end{pmatrix}$$

(a) You would like to determine a selling price for the cutting boards. What is the total cost of the wood for one cutting board of each style?

The cost of the wood for a cutting board of Style 1 is equal to the number of strips of each type of wood multiplied by the cost per strip, or

$$10(0.18) + 10(0.22) + 0(0.20) = 4.00.$$

The cost of the wood for a cutting board of Style 1 is \$4.00. This number was calculated by multiplying pairwise term by term the first row of B by the column in D. Using similar reasoning for Styles 2 and 3, we see that the matrix product BD gives the required information for each style.

$$
BD = \begin{array}{c} \\ 1 \\ 2 \\ 3 \end{array}
\begin{array}{ccc} o & w & c \\ \left(\begin{array}{ccc} 10 & 10 & 0 \\ 8 & 6 & 6 \\ 0 & 10 & 10 \end{array} \right) \end{array}
\begin{array}{c} o \\ w \\ c \end{array}
\begin{array}{c} Cost \\ \left(\begin{array}{c} 0.18 \\ 0.22 \\ 0.20 \end{array} \right) \end{array}
$$

$$
= \begin{array}{c} \\ 1 \\ 2 \\ 3 \end{array}
\begin{array}{c} Cost \\ \left(\begin{array}{c} 4.00 \\ 3.96 \\ 4.20 \end{array} \right) \end{array}
$$

The cost of the wood for a cutting board of Style 1 is \$4.00; the cost for Style 2 is \$3.96; and, for Style 3, the cost is \$4.20.

(b) You and your partner would like to know how much money to budget for purchasing the wood for the cutting boards. What are the total costs for you and your partner to produce the number of cutting boards listed in matrix A of Example 1?

The product AB from Example 1 gives the number of strips of wood used by you and your partner. Multiplying AB by D results in a matrix containing the costs for you and your partner, as shown below.

$$
(AB)(D) = \begin{array}{c} \\ You \\ Part \end{array}
\begin{array}{ccc} o & w & c \\ \left(\begin{array}{ccc} 112 & 164 & 84 \\ 108 & 176 & 116 \end{array} \right) \end{array}
\begin{array}{c} o \\ w \\ c \end{array}
\begin{array}{c} Cost \\ \left(\begin{array}{c} 0.18 \\ 0.22 \\ 0.20 \end{array} \right) \end{array}
$$

$$
= \begin{array}{c} \\ You \\ Part \end{array}
\begin{array}{c} Cost \\ \left(\begin{array}{c} 73.04 \\ 81.36 \end{array} \right) \end{array}
$$

The total cost for you is \$73.04; the total cost for your partner is \$81.36.

■

The rows and columns of data in the matrices in Examples 1 and 2 are described by labels. In matrix A, the row labels are names (you and your partner) and the column labels are styles of cutting board (1, 2, and 3), so that matrix A classifies data according to name and style; we refer to A as a name-by-style matrix. Consistent with this notation, matrix B is a style-by-wood matrix. The row and column labels of matrices are especially helpful in interpreting the results of matrix multiplication.

Observe that in Example 1 we multiplied a name-by-style matrix (A) by a style-by-wood matrix (B) to get a name-by-wood matrix (C). In Example 2, we multiplied a style-by-wood matrix (B) by a wood-by-cost matrix (D) to get a style-by-cost matrix. We also found that the product of a name-by-wood matrix (AB) and a wood-by-cost matrix (D) is a name-by-cost matrix. In each example, matrix multiplication eliminated the labels of the first factor's columns and the second factor's rows, leaving a product matrix with exactly the row and column labels we desired in our answer. Matrix multiplication, which at first glance seems very strange, actually is designed to give us the information we want in a straightforward manner.

A special type of matrix that appeared in Example 2 is a *vector*, a matrix that consists of either one column, called a column vector, or one row, called a row vector. In other branches of mathematics, a vector with n entries represents a point in n-dimensional space. For example, a vector with 3 entries can represent the x-, y-, and z-components of a geometric vector in 3-space.

Class Practice

The solutions to the following exercises contain information that is critical to subsequent concepts. The exercises should be investigated, and the solutions should be carefully reviewed.

1. What must be true of the dimensions of the matrices S and T if the product $U = ST$ is defined? If U is defined, what is its dimension? How does the relationship between the dimensions of S, T, and U relate to the labels of the row and column entries in each matrix? As used here, the term *defined* implies that the product exists and makes sense within the rules of matrix multiplication.

2. What is the result of a vector times a vector, assuming the multiplication is defined?

3. An *identity matrix* $I_{n \times n}$ is an $n \times n$ square matrix such that multiplying a matrix A by I returns A as the product (assuming A is of a dimension such that this operation is defined). For example, if we have the matrix

$$A = \begin{pmatrix} 1 & 2 \\ 3 & 4 \end{pmatrix},$$

then an identity matrix

$$I_{2 \times 2} = \begin{pmatrix} a & b \\ c & d \end{pmatrix}$$

possesses the property that $I_{2 \times 2} A = A$, or,

$$\begin{pmatrix} a & b \\ c & d \end{pmatrix} \begin{pmatrix} 1 & 2 \\ 3 & 4 \end{pmatrix} = \begin{pmatrix} 1 & 2 \\ 3 & 4 \end{pmatrix},$$

where a, b, c, and d are certain numbers. The preceding matrix product is equivalent to the following system of equations:

$$\begin{aligned} a + 3b &= 1 \\ 2a + 4b &= 2 \\ c + 3d &= 3 \\ 2c + 4d &= 4 \end{aligned}$$

What are the numbers a, b, c, and d of $I_{2 \times 2}$ that solve this system? What is $I_{3 \times 3}$? What is the general form of $I_{n \times n}$?

4. Is matrix multiplication commutative in general? In other words, is it always true that $AB = BA$? Is multiplication by the identity matrix commutative? According to your answers to these questions, is it necessary to use the terms *left-multiply* and *right-multiply* when referring to matrix multiplication? [Specifically, in the product AB, matrix A is right-multiplied by B, and B is left-multiplied by A.]

5. Suppose it takes you 2 hours to make each Style 1 cutting board, 2.5 hours for each of Style 2, and 3 hours for each of Style 3; your partner requires 0.75, 2, and 3.5 hours, respectively, for each of the three styles. Use matrix multiplication to determine the total amount of time you and your partner will each spend making all of the cutting boards in matrix A of Example 1.

Class Practice Answers

1. The number of columns of S must equal the number of rows of T. The product matrix U has the same number of rows as S and the same number of columns as T. In symbols,

$$S_{m \times n} T_{n \times p} = U_{m \times p}.$$

In addition, the column labels of S must be the same as the row labels of T, and U has the row labels of S and the column labels of T.

2. A row vector R times a column vector C yields the following:

$$\left(\begin{array}{cccc} r_1 & r_2 & \cdots & r_n \end{array} \right) \left(\begin{array}{c} c_1 \\ c_2 \\ \vdots \\ c_n \end{array} \right) = \left(\begin{array}{c} r_1 c_1 + r_2 c_2 + \cdots + r_n c_n \end{array} \right)$$

Note that the vectors must have the same number of entries for the multiplication to be defined, and that the product is a single number. [In other contexts, particularly in physics, this is the definition of the *scalar product* or *dot product* of two geometric vectors.]

If the order of multiplication is reversed, we have

$$\left(\begin{array}{c} c_1 \\ c_2 \\ \vdots \\ c_n \end{array} \right) \left(\begin{array}{cccc} r_1 & r_2 & \cdots & r_n \end{array} \right) = \left(\begin{array}{cccc} c_1 r_1 & c_1 r_2 & \cdots & c_1 r_n \\ c_2 r_1 & c_2 r_2 & \cdots & c_2 r_n \\ \vdots & \vdots & \vdots & \vdots \\ c_n r_1 & c_n r_2 & \cdots & c_n r_n \end{array} \right).$$

Although in this example of multiplying a column vector by a row vector, the numbers of entries in each vector are the same, this restriction is not necessary for the multiplication to be defined. In general, two forms exist for vector products, specifically,

$$R_{1 \times n} C_{n \times 1} = P_{1 \times 1},$$

and

$$C_{m \times 1} R_{1 \times n} = P_{m \times n}.$$

3. The identity matrices are the following:

$$I_{2\times 2} = \begin{pmatrix} 1 & 0 \\ 0 & 1 \end{pmatrix} \qquad I_{3\times 3} = \begin{pmatrix} 1 & 0 & 0 \\ 0 & 1 & 0 \\ 0 & 0 & 1 \end{pmatrix}$$

$$I_{n\times n} = \begin{pmatrix} 1 & 0 & \cdots & 0 & 0 \\ 0 & 1 & \cdots & 0 & 0 \\ \vdots & \vdots & \vdots & \vdots & \vdots \\ 0 & 0 & \cdots & 1 & 0 \\ 0 & 0 & \cdots & 0 & 1 \end{pmatrix}$$

The matrix $I_{n\times n}$ has 1's on the diagonal and 0's elsewhere.

4. Matrix multiplication is <u>not</u> commutative in general. Recall that in any product RS, the column labels of R must match the row labels of S. Reversing the order of multiplication may not be feasible because the definition of the product RS places no requirements on the row labels of R and the column labels of S, which must match if SR is defined. In fact, the number of rows of R may not equal the number of columns of S, thereby invalidating the product SR.

Even in a purely abstract example, in which the rows and columns are not assigned any labels, matrix multiplication is not generally commutative:

$$\begin{pmatrix} 1 & 3 \\ 2 & 0 \end{pmatrix} \begin{pmatrix} 3 & 1 \\ -1 & 0 \end{pmatrix} = \begin{pmatrix} 0 & 1 \\ 6 & 2 \end{pmatrix}$$

$$\begin{pmatrix} 3 & 1 \\ -1 & 0 \end{pmatrix} \begin{pmatrix} 1 & 3 \\ 2 & 0 \end{pmatrix} = \begin{pmatrix} 5 & 9 \\ -1 & -3 \end{pmatrix}$$

Multiplication by an identity matrix is commutative; however, the other matrix must be a square matrix. For example,

$$\begin{pmatrix} 1 & 2 \\ 3 & 4 \end{pmatrix} \begin{pmatrix} 1 & 0 \\ 0 & 1 \end{pmatrix} = \begin{pmatrix} 1 & 2 \\ 3 & 4 \end{pmatrix}$$

and

$$\begin{pmatrix} 1 & 0 \\ 0 & 1 \end{pmatrix} \begin{pmatrix} 1 & 2 \\ 3 & 4 \end{pmatrix} = \begin{pmatrix} 1 & 2 \\ 3 & 4 \end{pmatrix}.$$

5. We want to end up with a matrix that has two entries—time for you and time for your partner. A is a name-by-style matrix, so we should right-multiply A by a style-by-time matrix. Our answer is

$$\begin{array}{c} \\ You \\ Part \end{array} \begin{array}{cc} \begin{array}{ccc} 1 & 2 & 3 \end{array} \\ \begin{pmatrix} 8 & 4 & 6 \\ 6 & 6 & 8 \end{pmatrix} \end{array} \begin{array}{c} \\ 1 \\ 2 \\ 3 \end{array} \begin{array}{c} \begin{array}{cc} T_{you} & T_{part} \end{array} \\ \begin{pmatrix} 2.0 & 0.75 \\ 2.5 & 2.0 \\ 3.0 & 3.5 \end{pmatrix} \end{array} = \begin{array}{c} \\ You \\ Part \end{array} \begin{array}{c} \begin{array}{cc} T_{you} & T_{part} \end{array} \\ \begin{pmatrix} 44.0 & 35.0 \\ 51.0 & 44.5 \end{pmatrix} \end{array}.$$

Only the elements on the diagonal are meaningful in this problem. You require 44 hours and your partner requires 44.5 hours. The row 1, column 2 entry is the time required by your partner to make <u>your</u> cutting boards. The row 2, column 1 entry is the time you would need to make <u>your partner's</u> cutting boards.

3.1 Exercises

1. The following is a set of abstract matrices (without row and column labels):

$$M = \begin{pmatrix} 1 & -1 \\ 2 & 0 \end{pmatrix} \quad N = \begin{pmatrix} 2 & 4 & 1 \\ 0 & -1 & 3 \\ 1 & 0 & 2 \end{pmatrix} \quad O = \begin{pmatrix} 6 \\ -1 \end{pmatrix}$$

$$P = \begin{pmatrix} 0 & 1/2 \\ -1 & 1/2 \end{pmatrix} \quad Q = \begin{pmatrix} 4 \\ 1 \\ 3 \end{pmatrix} \quad R = \begin{pmatrix} 3 & 1 \\ -1 & 0 \end{pmatrix}$$

$$S = \begin{pmatrix} 3 & 1 \\ 1 & 0 \\ 0 & 2 \\ -1 & 1 \end{pmatrix} \quad T = \begin{pmatrix} 1 \\ 2 \\ -3 \\ 4 \end{pmatrix} \quad U = \begin{pmatrix} 4 & 2 & 6 & -1 \\ 5 & 3 & 1 & 0 \\ 0 & 2 & -1 & 1 \end{pmatrix}$$

   List all orders of pairs of matrices from this set for which the product is defined. State the dimension of each product.

2. Using the matrices M and P from Exercise 1 above, find the matrix products MP and PM. What property do you notice about these matrices?

3. Is matrix multiplication associative? In other words, is it always true that $A(BC) = (AB)C$, assuming these matrix products are defined? Use some of the matrices from Exercise 1 above to test your conjecture.

4. The K. L. Mutton Company has investments in three states—North Carolina, North Dakota, and New Mexico. Its deposits in each state are divided among bonds, mortgages, and consumer loans. The amount of money (in millions of dollars) invested in each category on June 1 is displayed in the table below.

	NC	ND	NM
Bonds	13	25	22
Mort.	6	9	4
Loans	29	17	13

   The current yields on these investments are 7.5% for bonds, 11.25% for mortgages, and 6% for consumer loans. Use matrix multiplication to find the total earnings for each state.

5. Several years ago Ms. Allen invested in growth stocks, which she hoped would increase in value over time. She bought 100 shares of stock A, 200 shares of stock B, and 150 shares of

stock C. At the end of each year she records the value of each stock. The table below shows the price per share (in dollars) of stocks A, B, and C at the end of the years 1984, 1985, and 1986.

	1984	1985	1986
Stock A	68.00	72.00	75.00
Stock B	55.00	60.00	67.50
Stock C	82.50	84.00	87.00

Calculate the total value of Ms. Allen's stocks at the end of each year.

6. A virus hits campus. Nurse Nancy discovers that students are either sick, well, or carriers of the virus. She finds the following percentages of people in each category, depending on whether they are a junior or a senior:

	Junior	Senior
Well	15%	25%
Sick	35%	40%
Carrier	50%	35%

The student population is distributed by class and sex as follows:

	Males	Females
Junior	104	80
Senior	107	103

How many sick males are there? How many well females? How many female carriers?

7. The Sound Company produces stereos. Their inventory includes four models—the Budget, the Economy, the Executive, and the President models. The Budget model needs 50 transistors, 30 capacitors, 7 connectors, and 3 dials. The Economy model needs 65 transistors, 50 capacitors, 9 connectors, and 4 dials. The Executive model needs 85 transistors, 42 capacitors, 10 connectors, and 6 dials. The President model needs 85 transistors, 42 capacitors, 10 connectors, and 12 dials. The daily manufacturing goal in a normal quarter is 10 Budget, 12 Economy, 11 Executive, and 7 President stereos.

   (a) How many transistors are needed each day? capacitors? connectors? dials?

   (b) During August and September, production is increased by 40%. How many Budget, Economy, Executive, and President models are produced daily during these months?

   (c) It takes 5 person-hours to produce the Budget model, 7 person-hours to produce the Economy model, 6 person-hours for the Executive model, and 7 person-hours for the President model. Determine the number of employees needed to maintain the normal production schedule, assuming everyone works an average of 7 hours each day. How many employees are needed in August and September?

8. [For students familiar with basic trigonometry.] The parabola $y = -4x^2 + 16x - 12$ contains the points (1,0), (2,4), and (3,0). Find the new ordered pairs x' and y' that are produced from (x, y) using the matrix multiplication below when $\theta = 30°$:

$$\begin{pmatrix} \cos\theta & -\sin\theta \\ \sin\theta & \cos\theta \end{pmatrix} \begin{pmatrix} x \\ y \end{pmatrix} = \begin{pmatrix} x' \\ y' \end{pmatrix}$$

Accurately plot the new points in the same coordinate system as the three given points of the original parabola. Sketch the remainder of the parabola as you think it would appear if every point on the original curve were transformed by the matrix multiplication above. Compare this sketch with a sketch of the original parabola. What happened? Try $\theta = 90°$ to test your conjecture.

9. The president of the Lucrative Bank is hoping for a 21% increase in checking accounts, a 35% increase in savings accounts, and a 52% increase in market accounts. The current statistics on the number of accounts at each branch are as follows:

	Checking	Savings	Market
Northgate	40039	10135	512
Downtown	15231	8751	105
South Square	25612	12187	97

What is the goal for each branch in each type of account? (HINT: multiply by a 3 × 3 matrix with certain nonzero entries on the diagonal and zero entries elsewhere.) What will be the total number of accounts at each branch?

10. Winners at a science fair are determined by a scoring system based on five items with different weights attached to each item. The items and associated weights are the summary of background research—weight 3; experimental procedure—weight 5; research paper—weight 6; project display—weight 8; and creativity of idea—weight 4. Each project is judged by grading each of the five items on a scale from 0 to 10, with 10 highest. The total score for a project is derived by adding the products of the corresponding weights and points for each item.

(a) What is the maximum total score possible for a project?

(b) Calculate the score for a student who earns 8 points on background research, 9 points on experimental procedure, 7 points on the research paper, 8 points on the project display, and 6 points on creativity.

(c) The table shown below contains the points for the finalists in the biology division. Calculate the total scores to determine the first, second, and third place entries.

	Peter	Jane	Bryan	Kathy	Mary	Chris	John
Background research	9	8	10	7	8	9	10
Experimental procedure	10	9	9	10	10	9	10
Research paper	7	9	8	9	7	8	8
Project display	9	10	9	8	10	8	9
Creativity of idea	8	7	8	10	6	8	7

11. The Metropolitan Opera is planning its last cross-country tour. It plans to perform *Carmen* and *La Traviata* in Atlanta in May. The person in charge of logistics wants to make plane reservations for the two troupes. *Carmen* has 2 stars, 25 other adults, 5 children, and 5 staff members. *La Traviata* has 3 stars, 15 other adults, and 4 staff members. There are 3 airlines to choose from. Piedmont charges round-trip fares to Atlanta of $630 for first class, $420 for coach, and $250 for youth. Eastern charges $650 for first class, $350 for coach, and $275 for youth. Air Atlanta charges $700 first class, $370 coach, and $150 youth. Assume stars travel first class, other adults and staff travel coach, and children travel for the youth fare.

   (a) Find the total cost for each opera troupe with each airline.

   (b) If each airline will give a 30% discount to the *Carmen* troupe because they will stay over Saturday, what is the total cost to the Met for each airline?

   (c) Suppose instead that each airline will give a discount to the Met just to get their business. Piedmont gives a 30% discount, Eastern 20%, and Air Atlanta 25%. Use matrix multiplication to find a new 3×3 cost matrix. (See the hint for Exercise 9.)

12. On the Sunday before the 1986 NCAA basketball finals, a survey was taken of people's choices to win the game, along with their income. The following information was collected:

   - 435 for Duke making over $30,000 per year
   - 105 for Louisville making over $30,000 per year
   - 115 with no choice making over $30,000 per year
   - 125 for Duke making under $30,000 per year
   - 205 for Louisville making under $30,000 per year
   - 231 with no choice making under $30,000 per year

   A survey was done in a bar in New York on the night of the game to determine the incomes of the people eating there (some were also watching the game). The following information was collected:

   - 302 making over $30,000 per year
   - 276 making under $30,000 per year

   Using matrix operations, estimate the number of Duke fans, the number of Louisville fans, and the number of fans with no choice in the bar, based on the survey from Sunday. These numbers are found using probabilities based on the Sunday survey and the data collected on the night of the game. Before you attempt to find an answer, the information from each survey should be converted to proportions and displayed in matrices.

13. A company that produces and markets stuffed animals has three plants—one on the East Coast, one on the West Coast, and one in the central part of the country. Among other items, each plant manufactures stuffed pandas, kangaroos, and rabbits. Personnel are needed to cut fabric, sew appropriate parts together, and provide finish work for each animal. Matrix *A* gives the time (in hours) of each type of labor required to make each type of stuffed animal;

matrix B gives the daily production capacity at each plant; matrix C provides hourly wages of the different workers at each plant; and matrix D contains the total orders received by the company in October and November.

$$A = \begin{array}{c} \\ Panda \\ Kangaroo \\ Rabbit \end{array} \begin{array}{ccc} Cutting & Sewing & Finishing \\ \left(\begin{array}{ccc} 0.5 & 0.8 & 0.6 \\ 0.8 & 1.0 & 0.4 \\ 0.4 & 0.5 & 0.5 \end{array} \right) \end{array}$$

$$B = \begin{array}{c} \\ East \\ Central \\ West \end{array} \begin{array}{ccc} Panda & Kangaroo & Rabbit \\ \left(\begin{array}{ccc} 25 & 15 & 12 \\ 10 & 20 & 15 \\ 20 & 15 & 15 \end{array} \right) \end{array}$$

$$C = \begin{array}{c} \\ East \\ Central \\ West \end{array} \begin{array}{ccc} Cutting & Sewing & Finishing \\ \left(\begin{array}{ccc} 7.50 & 9.00 & 8.40 \\ 7.00 & 8.00 & 7.60 \\ 8.40 & 10.50 & 10.00 \end{array} \right) \end{array}$$

$$D = \begin{array}{c} \\ Panda \\ Kangaroo \\ Rabbit \end{array} \begin{array}{cc} Oct & Nov \\ \left(\begin{array}{cc} 1000 & 1100 \\ 600 & 850 \\ 800 & 725 \end{array} \right) \end{array}$$

Use the matrices above to compute the following quantities:

(a) the hours of each type of labor needed each month (October, November) to fill all orders

(b) the production cost per item at each plant

(c) the cost of filling all October orders at the East Coast plant

(d) the daily hours of each type of labor needed at each plant if production levels are at capacity

(e) the daily amount each plant will pay its personnel when producing at capacity

4   The Leontief Input-Output Model and the Inverse of a Matrix

4.1   The Leontief Input-Output Model

We have seen that matrices are useful for organizing and manipulating data, and that the arithmetic of matrices makes sense in light of their applications. Another example of the use of matrices is in the Leontief Input-Output Model of an economy. In the April 1965 issue of *Scientific American*, Wassily Leontief explained his input-output system using the 1958 American economy. He divided the economy into 81 sectors grouped into 6 families, viewing the economy as a large 81×81 matrix. For his work, Leontief won the 1973 Nobel Prize for economics, and his model is now used worldwide. We will use a simplified version of his model to demonstrate the real-world importance of the inverse of a matrix.

Leontief divided the economy into 81 sectors (transportation, manufacturing, steel, utilities, etc.), each of which relies on input resources taken from the output of other sectors. For example, the steel industry uses the output of the utilities, heavy manufacturing, and transportation sectors, and even some steel, as inputs in its production. Therefore, not all steel is available to meet consumer demand; some steel, as well as other resources, is required for production of more steel. To develop the details of the Leontief model, we will examine a simplified economy that has only three sectors—agriculture, manufacturing, and transportation. The model hinges on the fact that some of the output from each sector is used in the production process, so that not all output is available to meet consumer demand.

The following technology information has been gathered by a research team:

- Production of a unit of output of agriculture requires inputs consisting of 1/10 of a unit of agriculture, 1/5 of a unit of manufacturing, and 1/5 of a unit of transportation. [A unit here refers to the value of a unit of output from the agriculture sector, where a unit can have some given monetary equivalence.]

- Production of a unit of output of manufacturing requires inputs consisting of 1/15 of a unit of agriculture, 1/4 of a unit of manufacturing, and 1/5 of a unit of transportation. [A unit here refers to the value of a unit of output from the manufacturing sector.]

- Production of a unit of output of transportation requires inputs consisting of no agriculture, 1/4 of a unit of manufacturing, and 1/6 of a unit of transportation. [A unit here refers to the value of a unit of output from the transportation sector.]

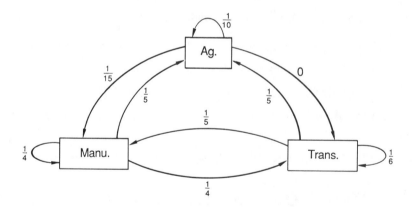

Figure 1: State Diagram for a Three-Sector Economy

The diagram in Figure 1, called a *state diagram*, illustrates the flow of resources from one sector to another. For example, the arc from manufacturing to transportation is assigned the number 1/4, indicating that the production of one unit of output of transportation requires the input of 1/4 of a unit of manufacturing. The arc from agriculture to agriculture is assigned the number 1/10, indicating that each unit of output of agriculture requires the input of 1/10 of a unit of agriculture. In general, an arc from sector i to sector j includes a number indicating the units of input required from sector i to produce one unit of output from sector j.

The matrix T reflecting this information, called the *technology matrix*, is shown below.

$$
\begin{array}{cccc}
 & Ag. & Manu. & Tran. \\
\begin{array}{c} Ag. \\ T = \ Manu. \\ Tran. \end{array} &
\left(\begin{array}{ccc}
1/10 & 1/15 & 0 \\
1/5 & 1/4 & 1/4 \\
1/5 & 1/5 & 1/6
\end{array} \right)
\end{array}
$$

For the sake of uniformity, the units of output for each sector are usually measured in dollars rather than physical units such as tons. Assuming a unit equals one dollar, from the matrix T above we observe that to produce one dollar's worth of manufactured goods requires about 7 cents worth (1/15 dollar) of agriculture, 25 cents worth of manufacturing, and 20 cents worth of transportation. In general, a column of the technology matrix gives the fraction of one dollar's worth of input from each sector needed to produce one dollar's worth of output in the sector represented by that column.

It is conventional, but not essential, for the column headings to represent output and for the row labels to represent input, as in matrix T above. The interpretations of rows and columns could be exchanged, but the matrix operations that we are about to describe would need to be modified in order to achieve correct results.

Suppose we know that the economy produces 100 million dollars worth of agriculture, 120 million dollars worth of manufacturing, and 120 million dollars worth of transportation. This information is displayed in the production matrix P shown below, in which the entries represent millions of dollars.

$$
\begin{array}{cc}
 & Prod. \\
\begin{array}{c} Ag. \\ P = \ Manu. \\ Tran. \end{array} &
\left(\begin{array}{c}
100 \\
120 \\
120
\end{array} \right)
\end{array}
$$

How much of each sector's output must be used to achieve the production levels given in matrix P? Since the output of each sector requires input produced in the other sectors, the total production is not available for the demands of consumers. Some of this production is consumed internally by the economy. By determining what resources are used in production, we will be able also to determine what amount remains for consumers. We will answer this question for each of the three sectors.

First, how many units of agriculture are used in the production of all three sectors? Each unit of agricultural output requires 0.1 units of agriculture as input; therefore, the 100 units of agriculture specified in P require $(1/10)(100)$ units of agriculture as input. Likewise, 120 units of manufacturing output require $(1/15)(120)$ units of agricultural input. The 120 units of transportation output require $(0)(120)$ units of agricultural input. The total input of agriculture necessary to meet the production levels given in P is thus given by

$$(\frac{1}{10})(100) + (\frac{1}{15})(120) + (0)(120) = 18 \text{ million dollars.}$$

How many units of manufacturing are used to produce at a level given by P? By the same reasoning as above, the total input of manufacturing required is

$$(\frac{1}{5})(100) + (\frac{1}{4})(120) + (\frac{1}{4})(120) = 80 \text{ million dollars.}$$

Finally, how many units of transportation are needed to achieve the production matrix P? Using the information in the technology matrix, we find that we require

$$(\frac{1}{5})(100) + (\frac{1}{5})(120) + (\frac{1}{6})(120) = 64 \text{ million dollars.}$$

In the calculations above, notice that the second factors in the products are the numbers found in P. The first factors in the expression for agriculture come from the agriculture row in the technology matrix. Likewise, the first factors in the expression for manufacturing come from the manufacturing row, and the first factors for transportation come from the transportation row. Clearly, the concept of matrix multiplication is at work in these calculations. In fact, the matrix product TP has entries corresponding to the calculations above, specifically,

$$TP = \begin{array}{c} Ag. \\ Manu. \\ Tran. \end{array} \overset{\begin{array}{ccc} Ag. & Manu. & Tran. \end{array}}{\begin{pmatrix} 1/10 & 1/15 & 0 \\ 1/5 & 1/4 & 1/4 \\ 1/5 & 1/5 & 1/6 \end{pmatrix}} \begin{array}{c} Ag. \\ Manu. \\ Tran. \end{array} \overset{Prod.}{\begin{pmatrix} 100 \\ 120 \\ 120 \end{pmatrix}}$$

$$= \begin{array}{c} Ag. \\ Manu. \\ Tran. \end{array} \begin{pmatrix} 18 \\ 80 \\ 64 \end{pmatrix}.$$

In general, if T is a technology matrix and P is a production matrix, then TP is a matrix that represents the amount of the output consumed by the system internally. The matrix that results from the product TP is called the *internal consumption matrix*. We observe that TP gives us the amount of each sector's output needed as input by the other sectors to meet production goals.

How much output is left to meet the demands of the consumers after the input requirements of each sector are met? This can be represented by the *demand matrix D* that is the difference between production and internal consumption. In symbols, D is defined as

$$D = P - TP.$$

Using the numbers provided above gives

$$\begin{array}{ccc} D & = & P - TP \end{array}$$

$$= \begin{array}{c} Ag. \\ Manu. \\ Tran. \end{array} \overset{Prod.}{\begin{pmatrix} 100 \\ 120 \\ 120 \end{pmatrix}} - \begin{array}{c} Ag. \\ Manu. \\ Tran. \end{array} \overset{Int.\,Cons.}{\begin{pmatrix} 18 \\ 80 \\ 64 \end{pmatrix}}$$

$$= \begin{array}{c} Ag. \\ Manu. \\ Tran. \end{array} \overset{Demand}{\begin{pmatrix} 82 \\ 40 \\ 56 \end{pmatrix}}.$$

The amounts left for distribution to consumers are 82 units of agriculture, 40 units of manufacturing, and 56 units of transportation, where a unit represents one million dollars.

Viewing this problem from a different perspective, we see that to have 82 units of agriculture available for consumer demand requires the production of 100 units of agriculture. Furthermore, to have 40 units of manufacturing available for demand, 120 units of manufacturing must be produced. To meet a demand of 56 units of transportation requires production of 120 units of transportation. Suppose the consumer demand for agriculture is not 82 units but is actually 100 units. What production goals must be set to meet this revised demand?

We have demonstrated a method for determining the quantity of resources available for consumer demand given a certain level of production. Generally, however, professional analysts will estimate society's demand for specific goods and services. The question usually investigated is the following: given a certain demand by society, how much should each sector of the economy produce in order to meet this demand? To produce less than the estimated demand may cause shortages and hardship; to produce more than the estimated demand leads to waste and inefficiency.

From the discussion above, we have $D = P - TP$. Since $P = IP$, where I is an identity matrix of the same dimension as T, this equation can be rewritten as

$$D = (I - T)P.$$

Because matrix multiplication is not commutative, P must be factored out to the right, since it is to the right of T. In this equation, we know the entries in the matrices D and $I - T$, and we wish to determine the matrix P.

The analogous situation with numbers is the equation

$$ax = b,$$

in which the values of a and b are known. To determine the value of x, we multiply both sides of the equation by the multiplicative inverse of a, namely $1/a$. This strategy transforms the equation as follows:

$$
\begin{aligned}
\frac{1}{a} \cdot a \cdot x &= \frac{1}{a} \cdot b \\
(\frac{1}{a} \cdot a) \cdot x &= \frac{1}{a} \cdot b \\
1 \cdot x &= b/a \\
x &= b/a
\end{aligned}
$$

The strategy in solving a matrix equation is similar. To isolate P on one side of the equation $D = (I - T)P$, we need to multiply both sides of the equation by the multiplicative inverse of $I - T$. The inverse of $I - T$ is a matrix that multiplies with the matrix $I - T$ to yield an identity matrix. (Refer back to the Class Practice in section 3 for an explanation of identity matrices.) Multiplying both sides of the equation $D = (I - T)P$ by the inverse of $I - T$ results in a right side that is the product of an identity matrix and P, or simply P. This process therefore isolates P so that economic production can be determined for a given amount of consumer demand.

Before going further with the problem of determining P, we need a method for finding the inverse of a matrix, which the following section explains.

4.2   Finding the Inverse of a Matrix

The inverse of a square matrix R is a matrix S such that the product of R and S is an identity matrix. For example, if

$$R = \begin{pmatrix} 1 & -1 \\ 2 & 0 \end{pmatrix} \quad \text{and} \quad S = \begin{pmatrix} 0 & 1/2 \\ -1 & 1/2 \end{pmatrix},$$

then

$$\begin{pmatrix} 1 & -1 \\ 2 & 0 \end{pmatrix} \begin{pmatrix} 0 & 1/2 \\ -1 & 1/2 \end{pmatrix} = \begin{pmatrix} 1 & 0 \\ 0 & 1 \end{pmatrix},$$

or

$$RS = I.$$

The matrices R and S are inverses of each other. The inverse of R is symbolized by R^{-1}, so that

$$R^{-1} = S,$$

and, likewise,

$$S^{-1} = R.$$

Given the matrix A shown below, what is the inverse of A?

$$A = \begin{pmatrix} a_{11} & a_{12} & a_{13} \\ a_{21} & a_{22} & a_{23} \\ a_{31} & a_{32} & a_{33} \end{pmatrix}$$

We wish to find a matrix such that when it is multiplied with A, the product is an identity matrix. In other words, what is the matrix A^{-1} such that $A^{-1}A = I$?

In approaching this problem, think of the entries in A as the coefficients of a system of linear equations. Specifically, the system of equations

$$\begin{aligned} a_{11}x_1 + a_{12}x_2 + a_{13}x_3 &= c_1 \\ a_{21}x_1 + a_{22}x_2 + a_{23}x_3 &= c_2 \\ a_{31}x_1 + a_{32}x_2 + a_{33}x_3 &= c_3 \end{aligned}$$

can be expressed as the matrix equation

$$\begin{pmatrix} a_{11} & a_{12} & a_{13} \\ a_{21} & a_{22} & a_{23} \\ a_{31} & a_{32} & a_{33} \end{pmatrix} \begin{pmatrix} x_1 \\ x_2 \\ x_3 \end{pmatrix} = \begin{pmatrix} c_1 \\ c_2 \\ c_3 \end{pmatrix}.$$

If we let

$$X = \begin{pmatrix} x_1 \\ x_2 \\ x_3 \end{pmatrix} \quad \text{and} \quad C = \begin{pmatrix} c_1 \\ c_2 \\ c_3 \end{pmatrix},$$

then the matrix equation above is equivalent to

$$AX = C.$$

Left-multiplying both sides of the equation above by the inverse of A provides the equivalent equation

$$A^{-1}AX = A^{-1}C.$$

Recall that since matrix multiplication is not commutative, both sides must be left-multiplied. This equation can be simplified to

$$IX = A^{-1}C,$$

so the solution for the X vector is

$$X = A^{-1}C.$$

When a system of equations is solved without introducing matrix notation, a common procedure for finding the solution involves transforming the system with the following operations:

1. Exchange the positions of two equations.

2. Multiply an equation by a nonzero constant.

3. Replace an equation with the sum of the equation and a multiple of another equation.

These operations each produce a system with a solution identical to that of the original system. Eventually a system results whose solution can be determined by inspection. This same strategy can be applied to the problem of finding the inverse of a matrix.

We can rewrite the matrix equation $AX = C$ in the equivalent form

$$AX = IC,$$

where I is an identity matrix of the same dimension as A. Suppose operations are performed on A and I that are equivalent to the manipulations performed on a system of equations. In other words, we manipulate the matrices A and I as we would the coefficients of a system of equations, performing the same operations on both sides of the matrix equation. If these operations eventually transform A into an identity matrix, then the left side of the matrix equation will be IX, or just X. Since X is on the left side, the right side of the equation will be $A^{-1}C$. To summarize, if we can transform A into I, then the same operations will transform I into A^{-1}.

The matrix operations analogous to the three transformations for systems of equations that can be used to find the inverse of a matrix are called *elementary row operations* (EROs). The three EROs are as follows:

1. Exchange two rows.

2. Multiply one row by a nonzero constant.

3. Replace a row with the sum of the row and a multiple of another row.

The use of EROs to determine the inverse of a matrix is demonstrated with the matrix A shown below.

$$A = \begin{pmatrix} 2 & 1 & 0 \\ 1 & 0 & 2 \\ 0 & 1 & -1 \end{pmatrix}$$

The goal is to transform A using EROs until we reach a 3×3 identity matrix. The inverse of A results from performing the same EROs on $I_{3\times3}$, so we write $I_{3\times3}$ alongside A. This form is called an *augmented matrix* and is shown below.

$$\begin{pmatrix} 2 & 1 & 0 & | & 1 & 0 & 0 \\ 1 & 0 & 2 & | & 0 & 1 & 0 \\ 0 & 1 & -1 & | & 0 & 0 & 1 \end{pmatrix}$$

We begin the sequence of EROs by interchanging rows 1 and 2 so that a 1 is in the upper left corner, which results in the new augmented matrix

$$\begin{pmatrix} 1 & 0 & 2 & | & 0 & 1 & 0 \\ 2 & 1 & 0 & | & 1 & 0 & 0 \\ 0 & 1 & -1 & | & 0 & 0 & 1 \end{pmatrix}.$$

Now add -2 times the first row to the second row.

$$\begin{pmatrix} 1 & 0 & 2 & | & 0 & 1 & 0 \\ 0 & 1 & -4 & | & 1 & -2 & 0 \\ 0 & 1 & -1 & | & 0 & 0 & 1 \end{pmatrix}$$

Already we are finished transforming the first column of A—it is identical to the first column of $I_{3\times3}$. Next add -1 times the second row to the third row, which finishes the second column, as shown below.

$$\begin{pmatrix} 1 & 0 & 2 & | & 0 & 1 & 0 \\ 0 & 1 & -4 & | & 1 & -2 & 0 \\ 0 & 0 & 3 & | & -1 & 2 & 1 \end{pmatrix}$$

To transform the third column, multiply the third row by $1/3$, yielding

$$\begin{pmatrix} 1 & 0 & 2 & | & 0 & 1 & 0 \\ 0 & 1 & -4 & | & 1 & -2 & 0 \\ 0 & 0 & 1 & | & -1/3 & 2/3 & 1/3 \end{pmatrix}.$$

Add 4 times row 3 to row 2, and add -2 times row 3 to row 1, leaving the matrix

$$\begin{pmatrix} 1 & 0 & 0 & | & 2/3 & -1/3 & -2/3 \\ 0 & 1 & 0 & | & -1/3 & 2/3 & 4/3 \\ 0 & 0 & 1 & | & -1/3 & 2/3 & 1/3 \end{pmatrix}.$$

The transformation process is now complete, and the inverse of A is

$$A^{-1} = \begin{pmatrix} 2/3 & -1/3 & -2/3 \\ -1/3 & 2/3 & 4/3 \\ -1/3 & 2/3 & 1/3 \end{pmatrix}.$$

Calculate the product of A^{-1} and A to verify that $A^{-1}A = I$.

Class Practice

The EROs performed above to find the inverse of A can also be accomplished through matrix multiplication, as the following exercises demonstrate.

1. The first ERO performed on A interchanged rows 1 and 2. Verify that the matrix

$$\begin{pmatrix} 0 & 1 & 0 \\ 1 & 0 & 0 \\ 0 & 0 & 1 \end{pmatrix}$$

interchanges rows 1 and 2 when A is left-multiplied by this matrix. What matrix will interchange rows 1 and 3? Rows 2 and 3?

2. Multiplying a row by a nonzero constant is a second ERO used to find the inverse of a matrix. Verify that left-multiplying A by the matrix

$$\begin{pmatrix} k & 0 & 0 \\ 0 & 1 & 0 \\ 0 & 0 & 1 \end{pmatrix}$$

multiplies the first row of A by k. What matrix will multiply row 2 by k? Row 3?

3. The third ERO involves multiplying a row by a constant k and adding it to another row. Verify that left-multiplying A by the matrix

$$\begin{pmatrix} 1 & k & 0 \\ 0 & 1 & 0 \\ 0 & 0 & 1 \end{pmatrix}$$

adds k times the second row of A to the first row of A in the result. What matrix will add k times the third row to the first row? k times row 2 to row 3?

4. List the 6 matrices that correspond to the 6 EROs used to find the inverse of A.

5. Find the product of the 6 matrices in Exercise 4, left-multiplying in order with the first ERO matrix being right-most, the second ERO matrix immediately to the left of the first, and so on. Notice that the result is A^{-1}.

6. Why must the ERO matrices be left-multiplied in Exercise 5 above? Is it possible to use right-multiplication?

4.2.1   Do All Matrices Have Inverses?

If A^{-1} is the inverse of A, then the inverse of A^{-1} is A, which means that

$$A \cdot A^{-1} = A^{-1} \cdot A = I.$$

Inverses can be multiplied in either of the two orders and the result will be an identity matrix, a property that can be verified with the entries in A and A^{-1}. An implication of this property is that only square matrices have inverses.

If a matrix has an inverse, it is said to be *invertible*. Are all square matrices invertible? If not, what are the general conditions for a square matrix A to have an inverse? Our method for finding an inverse involves using EROs to reduce matrix A to an identity matrix. If this is possible, then the same sequence of EROs will transform the identity matrix into A^{-1}. Recall that EROs were introduced as analogies of operations used to solve a system of linear equations, with A representing the coefficient matrix. If A is invertible, then the system can be solved with EROs; therefore, from the viewpoint of a linear system, the existence of A^{-1} is equivalent to the existence of a solution for the system $AX = C$. Asking the question of the invertibility of a matrix is equivalent to examining the question of the existence of a solution for a linear system.

Example 1: The equations in the 2-by-2 system

$$2x_1 + x_2 = 3$$
$$4x_1 + 2x_2 = 8$$

describe parallel lines because the coefficients of the second equation are twice the coefficients of the first equation, but the constant terms are not in a 2-to-1 ratio. This system has no solution. A system of linear equations that has no solution is called *inconsistent*.

The equations in the 2-by-2 system

$$3x_1 - x_2 = 5$$
$$9x_1 - 3x_2 = 15$$

both describe the same line because the coefficients and the constant term of the second equation are 3 times the corresponding numbers in the first equation. The system has an infinite number of solutions. A system of linear equations that has an infinite number of solutions is called *dependent*.

∎

If a linear system does not have a unique solution, then the matrix equation $AX = C$ that represents the system cannot be transformed to $X = A^{-1}C$; therefore, the coefficient matrix of an inconsistent or dependent system does not have an inverse. On the other hand, if a linear system represented by $AX = C$ does have a unique solution, the system is called *consistent* and A is invertible.

To find the inverse of a matrix, elementary row operations are used to transform the coefficient matrix A. If at any point in the process two rows of A are found to be equal, then A must not be invertible. What this means is that if any row of a matrix can be expressed as a sum of multiples of the other rows, then that matrix does not have an inverse. Adding multiples of rows is called *linear combination*. The property of a matrix that determines if it is invertible can be stated as follows: *A square matrix is invertible if and only if no row can be expressed as a linear combination of the other rows.*

Example 2: The first system from Example 1 above has a coefficient matrix

$$\begin{pmatrix} 2 & 1 \\ 4 & 2 \end{pmatrix}.$$

This matrix is not invertible because the second row is twice the first row.

In the matrix

$$\begin{pmatrix} 5 & -3 & 0 \\ 1 & 2 & -2 \\ 9 & -8 & 2 \end{pmatrix},$$

note that the third row is equal to twice the first row minus the second row, so that this matrix is not invertible.

■

4.2.2   Inverses That Are Difficult to Calculate

If the entries in a matrix A are close to the entries in a matrix B that is not invertible, then the inverse of A can be difficult to find using computer software. Computers have limited precision, meaning only a certain number of digits are stored in any series of calculations. The necessity for computers to round off calculations to the internal precision of the machine leads to a phenomenon called *round-off error*. In sequences of calculations such as inverting a matrix, round-off errors tend to increase as more calculations are completed. As we attempt to invert matrix A, within a few operations the computer will probably find A indistinguishable, or nearly so, from B, which does not have an inverse. In such a situation the computer would not be able to successfully find the inverse of A, or it would find an incorrect inverse. If computer software is used to compute the solution of a linear system, then the computer solution may need to be checked in the original system. A system of linear equations with a coefficient matrix that is close to a matrix that is not invertible is an example of what is called an *ill-conditioned* system. In general, an ill-conditioned system is one that is extremely sensitive to small changes in the values of coefficients of the system. A large change in the answer can result from a small change in a coefficient.

Example 3: This example illustrates the difficulties associated with an ill-conditioned system of linear equations. The system

$$\begin{aligned} 2x_1 + x_2 &= 3 \\ 1.9876x_1 + x_2 &= 6 \end{aligned}$$

has solutions $x_1 \approx -241.94$ and $x_2 \approx 486.87$. If the coefficients of this system are rounded to two decimal places, then the new system

$$\begin{aligned} 2x_1 + x_2 &= 3 \\ 1.99x_1 + x_2 &= 6 \end{aligned}$$

has solutions $x_1 = -300$ and $x_2 = 603$. A change in a coefficient by an amount 0.0014 causes a wild fluctuation in the solution. Rounding off 1.9876 to 1.99 leads to a solution quite different from the actual solution to the original system.

The system is ill-conditioned because it is close to the inconsistent system

$$\begin{aligned} 2x_1 + x_2 &= 3 \\ 2x_1 + x_2 &= 6, \end{aligned}$$

which is a system whose coefficient matrix is not invertible. Although a computer stores many more digits of a number than presented here, a computer does produce approximate values for calculations beyond its internal precision, and the difficulties of ill-conditioned systems thus arise.

■

4.3   Leontief's Model Revisited

Recall that Leontief's Input-Output Model gives the following relationship between consumer demand (D), the economy's production (P), and the input-output interaction between sectors stated by the technology matrix (T):

$$D = P - TP,$$

or

$$D = (I - T)P.$$

Each entry in the technology matrix T represents the output of one sector utilized as input by another sector. More specifically, the entry in row i and column j of T is the relative amount of goods and services needed as input from sector i for the production of the output resources of sector j. Although the technology matrix changes over time, the entries can be determined through research for a certain time period. The technology matrix from Section 4.1 is rewritten below with decimal numbers.

$$
T = \begin{array}{c} Ag. \\ Manu. \\ Tran. \end{array}
\begin{array}{ccc} Ag. & Manu. & Tran. \end{array}
\left(\begin{array}{ccc}
0.1 & 0.067 & 0 \\
0.2 & 0.25 & 0.25 \\
0.2 & 0.2 & 0.167
\end{array} \right)
$$

The entries of D are often estimated through market research. We wish to calculate a matrix P that will yield the given entries of D. To solve for the matrix P, left-multiply both sides of the equation $D = (I - T)P$ by the inverse of $(I - T)$ to give

$$(I - T)^{-1}D = (I - T)^{-1}(I - T)P,$$

which simplifies to

$$(I - T)^{-1}D = IP,$$

or

$$(I - T)^{-1}D = P.$$

Once again, notice the importance of maintaining the correct order of multiplication on both sides of the equation.

As displayed in the matrix below, suppose the consumer demand is for 100 units of agriculture, 120 units of manufacturing, and 90 units of transportation, where each unit represents one million dollars worth of a sector's goods.

$$
D = \begin{array}{c} Ag. \\ Manu. \\ Tran. \end{array}
\begin{array}{c} Dem. \end{array}
\left(\begin{array}{c}
100 \\
120 \\
90
\end{array} \right)
$$

Given this level of consumer demand, we wish to determine the level of production necessary to satisfy this demand as well as the amount of internal consumption given by the product TP.

The first step in calculating the matrix P is to determine $(I - T)^{-1}$. We start with

$$I - T = \begin{pmatrix} 1 & 0 & 0 \\ 0 & 1 & 0 \\ 0 & 0 & 1 \end{pmatrix} - \begin{pmatrix} 0.1 & 0.067 & 0 \\ 0.2 & 0.25 & 0.25 \\ 0.2 & 0.2 & 0.167 \end{pmatrix}$$

$$= \begin{pmatrix} 0.9 & -0.067 & 0 \\ -0.2 & 0.75 & -0.25 \\ -0.2 & -0.2 & 0.833 \end{pmatrix}$$

Using EROs and aided by computer software, we find that

$$(I - T)^{-1} \approx \begin{pmatrix} 1.14 & 0.11 & 0.03 \\ 0.43 & 1.49 & 0.45 \\ 0.38 & 0.38 & 1.32 \end{pmatrix}.$$

Now we can calculate P as follows:

$$\begin{aligned} P &= (I - T)^{-1}D \\ &\approx \begin{pmatrix} 1.14 & 0.11 & 0.03 \\ 0.43 & 1.49 & 0.45 \\ 0.38 & 0.38 & 1.32 \end{pmatrix} \begin{pmatrix} 100 \\ 120 \\ 90 \end{pmatrix} \\ &\approx \begin{matrix} Ag. \\ Manu. \\ Tran. \end{matrix} \begin{pmatrix} 129.9 \\ 262.3 \\ 202.4 \end{pmatrix} \end{aligned}$$

The economy must produce 129.9 million dollars worth of agriculture, 262.3 million dollars worth of manufacturing, and 202.4 million dollars worth of transportation to satisfy consumer demand after the requirements of internal consumption are met.

4.4   Exercises

1. Consider a 4-sector economic system consisting of petroleum, textiles, transportation, and chemicals. The production of 1 unit of petroleum requires 0.2 units of transportation, 0.4 units of chemicals, and 0.1 unit of itself. The production of 1 unit of textiles requires 0.4 units of petroleum, 0.1 unit of textiles, 0.15 units of transportation, and 0.3 units of chemicals. The production of 1 unit of transportation requires 0.6 units of petroleum, 0.1 unit of itself, and 0.25 units of chemicals. Finally, the production of 1 unit of chemicals requires 0.2 units of petroleum, 0.1 unit of textiles, 0.3 units of transportation, and 0.2 units of chemicals.

   (a) Write a technology matrix to represent this information.

   (b) On what sector is petroleum most dependent? Least dependent?

(c) If the textiles sector has an output of $4 million, what is the input in dollars from petroleum?

(d) Suppose the production matrix is

$$P = \begin{array}{c} Petr. \\ Text. \\ Tran. \\ Chem. \end{array} \begin{pmatrix} 800 \\ 200 \\ 700 \\ 750 \end{pmatrix}.$$

What is the internal consumption matrix? How much petroleum is left over for external use?

(e) Suppose the demand matrix, in millions of dollars, is

$$D = \begin{array}{c} Petr. \\ Text. \\ Tran. \\ Chem. \end{array} \begin{pmatrix} 25 \\ 14 \\ 30 \\ 42 \end{pmatrix}.$$

How much of each sector must be produced?

2. Suppose the demand matrix given in Exercise 1(e) is doubled. What is the new production matrix? How does the new production matrix compare with the original production matrix?

3. An economy with the four sectors manufacturing, petroleum, transportation, and hydroelectric power has the following technology matrix:

$$T = \begin{array}{c} Manu. \\ Petr. \\ Tran. \\ HP \end{array} \begin{array}{cccc} Manu. & Petr. & Tran. & HP \\ \begin{pmatrix} 0.15 & 0.18 & 0.3 & 0.1 \\ 0.22 & 0.12 & 0.37 & 0 \\ 0.09 & 0.3 & 0.11 & 0 \\ 0.27 & 0.05 & 0.07 & 0.1 \end{pmatrix} \end{array}$$

Find the production matrix if all the entries of the demand matrix are 200.

4. Consider a 3-sector system consisting of steel, coal, and transportation. The production of one unit of coal requires 0.23 units of transportation, 0.19 units of itself, and 0.2 units of steel. The production of 1 unit of steel requires 0.2 units of itself, 0.3 units of coal, and 0.15 units of transportation. Finally, producing 1 unit of transportation requires 0.1 units of itself, 0.15 units of coal, and 0.35 units of steel.

(a) Write a technology matrix to represent this information.

(b) On what sector does coal rely most? Rely least?

(c) Which sector depends most on steel?

(d) Suppose the production matrix is

$$P$$

$$
\begin{matrix}
Steel \\
Coal \\
Tran.
\end{matrix}
\begin{pmatrix}
18 \\
23 \\
15
\end{pmatrix}.
$$

What is the surplus available beyond internal consumption?

(e) Suppose the demand matrix is

$$D$$

$$
\begin{matrix}
Steel \\
Coal \\
Tran.
\end{matrix}
\begin{pmatrix}
24 \\
19 \\
12
\end{pmatrix}.
$$

Find the production matrix.

4.5 Additional Applications of the Inverse of a Matrix

Example: McDonald's is sponsoring special funding for three projects: scholarships for employees, special public service projects, and beautification of the exteriors of the restaurants. Each of the three locations of McDonald's in Durham made requests for funds, with the relative amounts requested by each location for the three projects distributed as shown in Table 2. Headquarters decided to allocate $100,000 for these projects to the Durham area. The money was to be distributed with 43% to scholarships, 28% to public service projects, and the remaining 29% to beautification. How much will each of the three restaurants receive?

Project	Location		
	Hillsborough	Northgate	Boulevard
Scholarships	50%	30%	40%
Public service	20%	30%	40%
Beautification	30%	40%	20%

Table 2: Distribution of Funding Requests

This problem can be approached by letting the variables x, y, and z stand for the amounts that each of the three restaurants will receive. A 3-by-3 system of equations based on the information in this problem can be written, and the system can then be solved by using matrices. Make the following variable assignments:

$$
\begin{aligned}
x &= \text{money for Hillsborough} \\
y &= \text{money for Northgate} \\
z &= \text{money for Boulevard}
\end{aligned}
$$

Each of the three projects leads to an equation in terms of x, y, and z, resulting in the following system of linear equations:

$$
\begin{aligned}
\text{Scholarships:} && 0.5x + 0.3y + 0.4z &= \$43{,}000 \\
\text{Public service:} && 0.2x + 0.3y + 0.4z &= \$28{,}000 \\
\text{Beautification:} && 0.3x + 0.4y + 0.2z &= \$29{,}000
\end{aligned}
$$

A matrix equation for this system is shown below.

$$
\begin{array}{c}
\\
Schol. \\
Pub.ser. \\
Beaut.
\end{array}
\begin{array}{ccc}
Hills. & North. & Blvd. \\
\left(\begin{array}{ccc}
0.5 & 0.3 & 0.4 \\
0.2 & 0.3 & 0.4 \\
0.3 & 0.4 & 0.2
\end{array} \right)
\end{array}
\begin{array}{c}
\\
H \\
N \\
B
\end{array}
\begin{array}{c}
Amt. \\
\left(\begin{array}{c}
x \\
y \\
z
\end{array} \right)
\end{array}
=
\begin{array}{c}
\\
Schol. \\
Pub.ser. \\
Beaut.
\end{array}
\begin{array}{c}
Amt. \\
\left(\begin{array}{c}
\$43{,}000 \\
\$28{,}000 \\
\$29{,}000
\end{array} \right)
\end{array}
$$

This matrix equation is of the form $AX = B$, so we can solve for X by finding A^{-1} and left-multiplying both sides, giving $X = A^{-1}B$. Substituting the entries of the matrices and using computer software to find the inverse of the coefficient matrix gives

$$
\begin{pmatrix} x \\ y \\ z \end{pmatrix} \approx
\begin{pmatrix}
3.333 & -3.333 & 0 \\
-2.667 & 0.667 & 4 \\
0.333 & 3.667 & -3
\end{pmatrix}
\begin{pmatrix}
\$43{,}000 \\
\$28{,}000 \\
\$29{,}000
\end{pmatrix}.
$$

After performing this multiplication, we find that

$$
\begin{pmatrix} x \\ y \\ z \end{pmatrix} =
\begin{pmatrix}
\$50{,}000 \\
\$20{,}000 \\
\$30{,}000
\end{pmatrix},
$$

in which the entries have been rounded to four significant digits. The \$100,000 should be distributed so that \$50,000 goes to the Hillsborough location, \$20,000 goes to the Northgate location, and \$30,000 goes to the Boulevard location.

■

For the preceding example, we did not actually need to know the entries in A^{-1}. All we are really interested in is the result of the multiplication $A^{-1}B$. Recall from the Class Practice exercises in section 4.2 that the EROs performed when finding A^{-1} can be represented by matrices, where the product of these matrices is A^{-1}. If we multiply B by these same ERO matrices, the result will be $A^{-1}B$; therefore, we can actually find the product $A^{-1}B$ by performing the same EROs on B that are performed on A in finding A^{-1}. In the example above, this is accomplished by first forming the augmented matrix

$$
\left(\begin{array}{ccc|c}
0.5 & 0.3 & 0.4 & 43{,}000 \\
0.2 & 0.3 & 0.4 & 28{,}000 \\
0.3 & 0.4 & 0.2 & 29{,}000
\end{array} \right),
$$

then using EROs to transform the left three columns into an identity matrix. The numbers in the right-hand column will be the solution to the system of equations found in the previous example.

4.6   Exercises

1. Explain why a matrix that contains a column of all zeros cannot have an inverse.

2. Solve the following systems using matrix algebra.

   (a) $2x - 5y + 7z = 4$
   $3x + y - 12z = -8$
   $5x + 2y - 4z = 3$

   (b) $2x - 5y + 7z = 4$
   $3x + y - 12z = -8$
   $5x - 4y - 5z = -4$

   (c) $2x - 5y + 7z = 4$
   $3x + y - 12z = -8$
   $7x - 9y + 2z = 1$

3. Find the inverses of the following matrices.

   (a) $\begin{pmatrix} 2 & -7 & 5 \\ 1 & -3 & -10 \\ 3 & 4 & -5 \end{pmatrix}$ (b) $\begin{pmatrix} 1 & 2 & 4 & 8 \\ 1 & 3 & 9 & 27 \\ 1 & 4 & 16 & 64 \\ 1 & 5 & 25 & 125 \end{pmatrix}$

4. Suppose that the Hillsborough location changes its request to McDonald's by asking for 43% for scholarships, 28% for public service, and 29% for beautification, using the same allocation scheme as the headquarters did. The other stores keep their original requests. How much money will each store receive?

5. The snack bar makes two types of sandwiches. The chicken sandwich takes 6 minutes to cook and 2 minutes to put on a bun with the lettuce, tomato, and mayonnaise. The hamburger takes 4 minutes to cook and 3 minutes to put on a bun with the tomato, lettuce, and mustard. How many hamburgers and chicken sandwiches can be produced if 40 minutes is spent on cooking and 20 minutes on preparing the sandwiches? How many hamburgers and chicken sandwiches can be produced with 35 minutes spent on cooking and 25 on preparing the sandwiches? How many with 45 minutes spent on cooking and 15 minutes spent preparing the sandwiches?

6. In section 3.1, Exercise 8, we found that the matrix below rotates a point (x, y) through an angle θ. Find the inverse of this matrix. What operation does it perform?

$$\begin{pmatrix} \cos\theta & -\sin\theta \\ \sin\theta & \cos\theta \end{pmatrix}$$

7. A total of $30,000 is available in a school for student groups to spend on their projects. The Student Council, the Beta Club, and the 4-H Club were asked to submit proposals describing how they would spend their portion of the $30,000. The principal accepted the following proposals for how each group would spend its allocation of the money:

	Activities	Community service	Club expenses
Student Council	40%	40%	20%
Beta Club	20%	50%	30%
4-H Club	20%	30%	50%

(a) The principal wants to allocate 30% of the funds to activities, 50% to community service, and 20% to club expenses. How much money would each club receive under these conditions? What problem results from this allocation?

(b) Assuming the principal's allocation scheme in part (a), how much would each club receive if the Beta Club changed its proposal so that it would spend 30% on activities, 50% on community services, and 20% on club expenses?

(c) The principal actually decides to allocate 25% of the funds to activities, 40% to community service, and 35% to club expenses. On the basis of the original proposals from each group, how much money does the principal allocate to each group?

5   The Leslie Matrix Model

Population growth is a significant phenomenon for which many mathematical models have been developed. A frequently used model is the exponential function

$$P(t) = P_0 e^{kt},$$

in which $P(t)$ is a population growing without limits. Constrained growth of a population can be modeled by the logistic growth function. The logistic equation is

$$P(t) = \frac{QM}{Q + e^{-kt}},$$

in which M is the maximum sustainable population and

$$Q = \frac{P_0}{M - P_0}$$

is the ratio of the initial population to the room for growth. Both of these models are macromodels, meaning that the models consider the population as a whole. In this section, a micromodel is developed that allows us to investigate questions about the different age groups within an entire population.

5.1   Modeling Age-Specific Population Growth

The future of social security, the future of veteran's benefits, and the changing school population in different regions of the country are current issues in public policy. The principal question arising in each of these discussions is how many people will be of a certain age after a period of time. The total population can be modeled with the equations above, but macromodels provide little help in answering age-specific growth questions. We would like to be able to examine the growth and decline of future populations according to various age groups. The model developed in this section will enable us to make these age-specific projections.

A fundamental assumption we will use in our model is that the proportion of males in the population is the same as the proportion of females, an assumption largely justified for most species. Consider a female population of small woodland mammals; Table 3 gives the populations for 3-month age groups. The total population in each age group is assumed to be twice the female population. The life span of this mammal is assumed to be 15–18 months, so none advance beyond the final column in Table 3. Our primary task with this data is to derive a mathematical model that will allow us to predict the number of animals in each age group after some number of years. To proceed, we first need to know something about the birth rate and death rate for each age group, rates that vary with age for most animal populations.

Age (months)	0–3	3–6	6–9	9–12	12–15	15–18
Number of females	14	8	12	4	0	0

Table 3: A Population of Small Woodland Mammals

The birth rate depends on a variety of factors, such as the probability that an animal will become pregnant, the number of pregnancies that can occur in any age group, and the average number of newborns in a litter. For animals that bear only one young and require a long gestation period, the birth rate is low; however, for insects, fish, and other species that bear thousands of young at a time, the birth rate is large.

Generally, the birth rate is given as a proportion of the total population. For example, if an animal population of 100 has a birth rate of 0.4, then it is understood that the 100 animals will produce 40 newborns, or 0.4 of the population. If we consider only the female population, the 50 females of the 100 animals (half of the total) will be reproducing at a rate of 0.8 of their population, since the 50 females will produce 40 young. Only 20 of these 40 young are expected to be female, however, so the birth rate of females would be 0.4 of the female population. In our model, the birth rate will represent the average number of daughters born to each female in the population during a specified time interval. Under the assumption of equal female and male proportions, this definition of birth rate is equivalent to viewing birth rate as a proportion of the total population.

For the species with the age distribution given in Table 3, the birth rate and death rate by age are listed in Table 4.

Rate	Age (months)					
	0–3	3–6	6–9	9–12	12–15	15–18
Birth rate	0	0.3	0.8	0.7	0.4	0
Death rate	0.4	0.1	0.1	0.2	0.4	1

Table 4: Birth Rate and Death Rate for Each Age Group

To investigate the mammal population in each age group over time, we begin by considering the following question: After 3 months, how many females will there be in each age group?

The populations of age groups 3–6, 6–9, 9–12, and 12–15 are easily found. The calculations can be simplified by introducing a quantity called the survival rate (SR), which is equal to one minus the death rate (DR). In symbols, the relationship is

$$SR = 1 - DR.$$

Whereas the death rate indicates the proportion of a population group that dies in a 3-month interval, the survival rate is the proportion of a population group that survives a 3-month period. The survival rate of the 0–3 age group is 0.6 ($= 1 - 0.4$), and the number of mammals from the original 14 that advance to the 3–6 age group after 3 months is

$$(0.6)(14) = 8.4.$$

The survival rate of the 3–6 age group is 0.9 ($= 1 - 0.1$), and of the original 8 mammals in this group, the number that advance to the 6–9 age group after 3 months is

$$(0.9)(8) = 7.2.$$

The calculations for the number of mammals moving up to the next age group after 3 months are summarized in Table 5.

Age	DR	SR	Number	Number moving up
0–3	0.4	0.6	14	$(0.6)(14) \Rightarrow 8.4$ move up to the 3–6 age group
3–6	0.1	0.9	8	$(0.9)(8) \Rightarrow 7.2$ move up to the 6–9 age group
6–9	0.1	0.9	12	$(0.9)(12) \Rightarrow 10.8$ move up to the 9–12 age group
9–12	0.2	0.8	4	$(0.8)(4) \Rightarrow 3.2$ move up to the 12–15 age group
12–15	0.4	0.6	0	$(0.6)(0) \Rightarrow 0$ move up to the 15–18 age group
15–18	1	0	0	no animal advances beyond the 15–18 group

Table 5: Movement of Females Up through Age Groups

The numbers in Table 5 may seem strange because the populations are not rounded to integers but contain fractional parts. These fractions of animals should remain in our analysis. The birth rates and survival rates used in the model are probabilistic quantities. They represent the probable rates for a given time, perhaps found by averaging data on a species for a number of years. We would not expect these rates to be exact at any one time, but we expect that over the long run they accurately reflect age-specific population growth. The fractional parts can make a significant difference in calculations over time, so they must be retained. To obtain an estimate of the population at a definite time, or a "snapshot" of the process, one would of course round off numbers to the nearest integer.

A question we have left unanswered is how many females enter the 0–3 age group. This is the sum of all the births in each of the other age groups. To find the births in each age group, multiply the birth rate times the population in that age group. Using the data from Table 4, this sum is

$$14(0) + 8(0.3) + 12(0.8) + 4(0.7) + 0(0.4) + 0(0) = 0 + 2.4 + 9.6 + 2.8 + 0 + 0$$
$$= 14.8.$$

Consolidating this number with the information in Table 5 gives us the female population in each age group after 3 months, as presented in Table 6. Notice that the population has grown from 38 to about 44 animals after 3 months.

Age	0–3	3–6	6–9	9–12	12–15	15–18
Number	14.8	8.4	7.2	10.8	3.2	0

Table 6: Female Population after Three Months

After another 3-month period, how many females will be in each group? Sixty percent of the 14.8 females in the 0–3 age group, or 8.88 females, will survive to move into the 3–6 age group. Of the 8.4 females in the 3–6 age group, ninety percent (7.56) will survive to move into the 6–9 age bracket. Ninety percent of the 7.2 females in the 6–9 age bracket, or 6.48 females, will survive to move into the 9–12 age group, while eighty percent (8.64) of the 10.8 females in the 9–12 age group will survive. Of the 3.2 females in the 12–15 age group, sixty percent (1.92) will move into the 15–18 age group. The 0–3 age group will be populated by newborns from each group. The total moving into the 0–3 age group will be

$$14.8(0) + 8.4(0.3) + 7.2(0.8) + 10.8(0.7) + 3.2(0.4) + 0(0) = 17.12.$$

Table 7 shows the number of animals in the female population after 6 months. The total population of females is now about 51, which implies, by the equal-proportions assumption, that the total animal population has reached about 102.

Age	0–3	3–6	6–9	9–12	12–15	15–18
Number	17.12	8.88	7.56	6.48	8.64	1.92

Table 7: Female Population after Six Months

Class Practice

1. Find the total population of females after 9 months.

2. Find the total population of females after 12 months.

5.2   The Leslie Matrix

In the previous example, we saw an increase in the population from 38 to about 44 during the initial 3-month interval, followed by an increase to about 51 after 6 months. Further calculations reveal that the population remains around 51–52 for the next two cycles, 9 and 12 months. During subsequent intervals will the population remain stable around 51, begin to grow again, or start to die out? We can answer this question by performing the same sequence of operations to calculate the population every 3 months; however, the matrix data structure provides an easier way to determine future age-specific population distributions.

The form of the calculations of Section 5.1 provides clues for developing a matrix model of age-specific population growth. The sums of products that were used in the calculations of Section 5.1

can each be represented as a row of one matrix times a column of another matrix. We will develop a matrix representation for the data that determine the age distribution of a population from one interval to the next, namely the birth rates and survival rates. This matrix is called the *Leslie matrix*, and will be symbolized by L. The survival rate for the kth age group is denoted by S_k. Similarly, denote the birth rate for the initial age group (0–3 months) by B_1, the next (3–6 months) by B_2, and, in general, the birth rate of the kth age group by B_k.

The number of females in each age group can be represented by a column vector called an *age distribution vector*. In our example, we have

$$
X_0 = \begin{pmatrix} 14 \\ 8 \\ 12 \\ 4 \\ 0 \\ 0 \end{pmatrix}
\quad \text{and} \quad
X_1 = \begin{pmatrix} 14.8 \\ 8.4 \\ 7.2 \\ 10.8 \\ 3.2 \\ 0 \end{pmatrix}
$$

where the subscript of X signifies the number of 3-month intervals that have elapsed. X_0 was given and X_1 was calculated based on X_0 and the birth rates and survival rates.

The first entry in X_1 was obtained by multiplying the values in X_0 times the birth rates for the n different age groups. If the first row of L is

$$
\begin{pmatrix} B_1 & B_2 & B_3 & B_4 & \cdots & B_n \end{pmatrix},
$$

then multiplying the first row of L with the column vector X_0 will yield the first entry in X_1. The second entry in X_1 is the product of the survival rate for the first age group and the number of females in the first age group from the previous cycle, which is the first entry in X_0. If the second row of L is

$$
\begin{pmatrix} S_1 & 0 & 0 & 0 & \cdots & 0 \end{pmatrix},
$$

then multiplying this by X_0 will provide the second entry in X_1. The third entry in X_1 is the product of the survival rate for the second age group and the number of females in the second age group from the previous cycle, which is the second entry in X_0. If the third row of L is

$$
\begin{pmatrix} 0 & S_2 & 0 & 0 & \cdots & 0 \end{pmatrix},
$$

then the result of multiplying this row by X_0 is the third entry in X_1.

This pattern is continued for the remaining rows of L; therefore, the Leslie matrix L is defined as

$$
L = \begin{pmatrix}
B_1 & B_2 & B_3 & B_4 & \cdots & B_{n-1} & B_n \\
S_1 & 0 & 0 & 0 & \cdots & 0 & 0 \\
0 & S_2 & 0 & 0 & \cdots & 0 & 0 \\
0 & 0 & S_3 & 0 & \cdots & 0 & 0 \\
\vdots & \vdots & \vdots & \vdots & & \vdots & \vdots \\
0 & 0 & 0 & 0 & \cdots & S_{n-1} & 0
\end{pmatrix}.
$$

For the woodland mammal example given in Section 5.1, we have

$$
L = \begin{pmatrix}
0 & 0.3 & 0.8 & 0.7 & 0.4 & 0 \\
0.6 & 0 & 0 & 0 & 0 & 0 \\
0 & 0.9 & 0 & 0 & 0 & 0 \\
0 & 0 & 0.9 & 0 & 0 & 0 \\
0 & 0 & 0 & 0.8 & 0 & 0 \\
0 & 0 & 0 & 0 & 0.6 & 0
\end{pmatrix}.
$$

Why have we chosen the definition of the Leslie matrix explained above? To see the rationale for the definition, examine the product LX_0 shown below.

$$
\begin{aligned}
LX_0 &= \begin{pmatrix}
0 & 0.3 & 0.8 & 0.7 & 0.4 & 0 \\
0.6 & 0 & 0 & 0 & 0 & 0 \\
0 & 0.9 & 0 & 0 & 0 & 0 \\
0 & 0 & 0.9 & 0 & 0 & 0 \\
0 & 0 & 0 & 0.8 & 0 & 0 \\
0 & 0 & 0 & 0 & 0.6 & 0
\end{pmatrix}
\begin{pmatrix}
14 \\ 8 \\ 12 \\ 4 \\ 0 \\ 0
\end{pmatrix} \\
&= \begin{pmatrix}
0(14) + 0.3(8) + 0.8(12) + 0.7(4) + 0.4(0) + 0(0) \\
0.6(14) + 0(8) + 0(12) + 0(4) + 0(0) + 0(0) \\
0(14) + 0.9(8) + 0(12) + 0(4) + 0(0) + 0(0) \\
0(14) + 0(8) + 0.9(12) + 0(4) + 0(0) + 0(0) \\
0(14) + 0(8) + 0(12) + 0.8(4) + 0(0) + 0(0) \\
0(14) + 0(8) + 0(12) + 0(4) + 0.6(0) + 0(0)
\end{pmatrix} \\
&= \begin{pmatrix}
14.8 \\ 8.4 \\ 7.2 \\ 10.8 \\ 3.2 \\ 0
\end{pmatrix}
\end{aligned}
$$

The matrix above is just X_1; thus, the form of the Leslie matrix leads to the matrix equation $LX_0 = X_1$.

Class Practice

1. Verify that $LX_k = X_{k+1}$ for $k = 1$, 2, and 3 by comparing these products with the values shown in the text and the Class Practice exercises of Section 5.1.

2. Verify that $L^k X_0 = X_k$ for $k = 1$, 2, 3, and 4 by comparing these products with the X_k vectors evaluated previously. L^k is defined as the matrix L raised to the kth power, or in other words, L multiplied by itself k times.

The Leslie matrix has been defined so that left-multiplication by it will generate the age distribution vectors in the sequence $X_0, X_1, \ldots, X_{k-1}, X_k$, as shown in the first Class Practice exercise above. Multiplication by L determines the next successive age distribution vector from the current vector; however, we need not go through all of the $k - 1$ preceding vectors just to find the kth vector. Since we always left-multiply X_{k-1} by L to find X_k, the associative property of matrix multiplication implies that we can simply multiply L by itself k times (which is L^k) and then right-multiply the result by the initial age distribution vector X_0. This property was demonstrated in the second Class Practice exercise above and is shown in general in the calculations below.

We have observed that

$$X_1 = LX_0$$

and

$$X_2 = LX_1.$$

By substitution of the first expression for X_1 into the second equation, we find that

$$\begin{aligned} X_2 &= L(LX_0) \\ &= L^2X_0. \end{aligned}$$

Similarly, substitution of the expression for X_2 into the equation

$$X_3 = LX_2$$

yields

$$\begin{aligned} X_3 &= L(L^2X_0) \\ &= L^3X_0. \end{aligned}$$

In general, we have the following sequence of equivalent expressions:

$$\begin{aligned} X_k &= LX_{k-1} \\ &= L(LX_{k-2}) \\ &= L(L(L\cdots(LX_0)\cdots)) \\ &= (L(L(L\cdots L)\cdots))X_0 \\ &= L^kX_0 \end{aligned}$$

An interesting pattern emerges in the long-term behavior of a process modeled with the Leslie matrix. The total female population of the woodland mammals is shown below for the first 5 cycles (a total elapsed time of 15 months).

Cycle	0	1	2	3	4	5
Female population	38	44.4	50.6	52.14	51.33	53.76

No obvious pattern is apparent from examining the total female population during the first 5 cycles; however, a pattern does emerge further along in the process. The total female population during cycles 10–13 increases by a gradually larger percent as shown in the table below.

Cycle	10	11	12	13
Female population	62.7874	64.5985	66.5059	68.5738
Percent growth		2.88	2.95	3.11

Does the percentage growth of the population during each cycle continue to increase? Moving even further along in the process sheds light on this question. The results of calculations for cycles 20–23 are shown below.

Cycle	20	21	22	23
Female population	84.5867	87.1639	89.8168	92.5485
Percent growth		3.05	3.04	3.04

The growth rate appears to be stabilizing at about 3.04% per 3-month cycle. After 30 cycles, the total female population is 114.158, and after 31 cycles, it is 117.632—an increase of 3.04%. Additional calculations confirm that the growth rate of the population converges to about 3.04%. This is called the *long-term growth rate* of the total population. The growth rate of the total population after a small number of cycles, called the *short-term growth rate*, is variable and does not reveal a pattern. After a large number of cycles, however, a stable long-term growth rate appears.

Examination of the age distribution vector X_k for large k also leads to some interesting results. The age distributions of the population after 20 and 21 cycles are

$$X_{20} = \begin{pmatrix} 27.46 \\ 15.99 \\ 13.97 \\ 12.20 \\ 9.47 \\ 5.51 \end{pmatrix} \quad \text{and} \quad X_{21} = \begin{pmatrix} 28.29 \\ 16.47 \\ 14.39 \\ 12.57 \\ 9.76 \\ 5.68 \end{pmatrix}.$$

The total female population after 20 cycles is 84.60, and after 21 cycles is 87.16. If the entries in an age distribution vector are each divided by the current total female population, then the resulting entries are the proportions of the total population found in each age group at that time. If each entry in X_{20} is divided by the total female population 84.60 and each entry in X_{21} is divided by the total female population 87.16, then the proportions found are

$$X_{20}/84.60 = \begin{pmatrix} 0.3246 \\ 0.1890 \\ 0.1651 \\ 0.1442 \\ 0.1119 \\ 0.0651 \end{pmatrix} \quad \text{and} \quad X_{21}/87.16 = \begin{pmatrix} 0.3246 \\ 0.1890 \\ 0.1651 \\ 0.1442 \\ 0.1120 \\ 0.0652 \end{pmatrix}.$$

The proportion of the population in each age group appears to reach a stable distribution. Examining the data after cycles 30 and 31, we find that the differences in the proportions from X_{30} to X_{31} are less than 10^{-6}. In the long run, therefore, the woodland mammal population tends to the following approximate distribution: 32% are 0–3 months old, 19% are 3–6 months old, 17% are 6–9 months old, 14% are 9–12 months old, 11% are 12–15 months old, and 7% are 15–18 months old.

A final property of the Leslie matrix model concerns the growth rates of the different age groups. Since the long-term proportions in each age group are fixed, and the growth rate of the total population eventually remains at 3.04%, then the growth rate of each age group must also eventually converge to 3.04%. This implies that for a large enough value of k, the age distribution vector X_k is equal to the scalar 1.0304 times the previous age distribution vector X_{k-1}. In symbols, we have that eventually, for large k,

$$X_k = 1.0304 X_{k-1}.$$

In the calculations above, we have seen evidence of the following general characteristics of the long-term behavior of the Leslie matrix model:

1. The growth rate of the total population converges to a constant percentage growth rate, called the long-term growth rate.

2. The proportions of the population in each age group eventually approach fixed values, and the growth rate of each age group stabilizes at the same value as the long-term growth rate of the total population.

3. For large k, successive age distribution vectors are related by

$$X_k = (1+r)X_{k-1},$$

where r is the long-term growth rate.

5.3   Exercises

1. Using the data from section 5.1, how many mammals will be in the 6–9 month age group in 5 years? In 10 years?

2. How long will it take for the total number of mammals to exceed 500? Note: Instead of adding up the entries in an age distribution vector by hand to find the total population, matrix software will conveniently provide the total population if the age distribution vector is left-multiplied by the row vector

$$\begin{pmatrix} 1 & 1 & \cdots & 1 \end{pmatrix}.$$

3. For each initial age distribution vector given below, use the Leslie matrix from the woodland mammal example to determine the length of time before the total population reaches 500.

$$\text{(a)} \quad X_0 = \begin{pmatrix} 20 \\ 10 \\ 8 \\ 0 \\ 0 \\ 0 \end{pmatrix} \qquad \text{(b)} \quad X_0 = \begin{pmatrix} 38 \\ 0 \\ 0 \\ 0 \\ 0 \\ 0 \end{pmatrix} \qquad \text{(c)} \quad X_0 = \begin{pmatrix} 6 \\ 6 \\ 6 \\ 6 \\ 6 \\ 8 \end{pmatrix}$$

4. For each of the initial age distributions given in Exercise 3, determine the long-term growth rate of the total population. Use the same Leslie matrix. How does the initial age distribution appear to be related to the long-term growth rate?

5. Using the Leslie matrix from the woodland mammal example, compare the long-term proportions of the population in each age group for the initial age distribution vectors

$$X_0 = \begin{pmatrix} 20 \\ 15 \\ 10 \\ 0 \\ 0 \\ 0 \end{pmatrix} \quad \text{and} \quad X_0 = \begin{pmatrix} 22 \\ 16 \\ 12 \\ 9 \\ 8 \\ 10 \end{pmatrix}.$$

Form a conjecture based on your results.

6. Suppose an animal population has the characteristics described in the table below.

Rates	Age group (years)						
	0–5	5–10	10–15	15–20	20–25	25–30	30–35
Birth	0	0	1.2	0.8	0.7	0.2	0
Death	0.5	0.2	0.1	0.1	0.3	0.5	1

(a) What is the expected life span of this animal?

(b) Construct the Leslie matrix for this animal.

(c) For the initial female population given in the table shown below, find the female age distribution and the total female population after 300 years.

Age group	0–5	5–10	10–15	15–20	20–25	25–30	30–35
Number	30	30	26	28	32	15	10

(d) Determine the long-term growth rate for this population.

(e) If the maximum sustainable population for this animal in its native habitat is 700, when will the maximum population be reached?

5.4   Exponential Growth and Harvesting

Uninhibited population growth is usually exponential because the population typically grows by a constant percentage of the existing population. We have observed with the Leslie matrix model that the overall population eventually grows by a constant percentage rate, leading to exponential growth. In reality, however, uninhibited growth does not continue indefinitely. In time, scarcity of resources will cause a population to stabilize or even to decline, perhaps through disease or starvation. To avoid the effects produced by overpopulation of a habitat, the growth of an animal population can be decreased by artificially removing a portion of the population during each specified time interval. This process is known as *harvesting*. In this section, we will investigate what harvesting rate should be used to stabilize a population. In other words, we will determine a harvesting strategy that results in a zero rate of population growth.

The mathematical model for this problem is simplified if we assume that the same percentage of animals will be removed from each age group, a process called *uniform harvesting*. With domesticated animals, uniform harvesting is clearly feasible; however, in the wild, animal populations are harvested by allowing a certain number of animals to be hunted. If no age or sex restrictions are set on the hunting of the animals, then we can assume that animals will be hunted randomly, thus resulting in uniform harvesting. Although this assumption may not be entirely justified (for example, the very young may not be hunted as much as older animals), it greatly simplifies the mathematics involved in our analysis. With some adjustment, we can use the Leslie matrix model to investigate the effects of uniform harvesting.

Under the assumption of uniform harvesting, suppose a proportion h of each age group of a population is harvested. This means that $1 - h$ of the population that would normally survive a cycle actually advances to the next cycle. For example, if 0.3 of the animals are harvested ($h = 0.3$) during each cycle, then 0.7 of the animals in each age group that normally survive would actually advance to a higher age group for the next cycle. If an age group has a survival rate of 0.9 without harvesting, then a harvesting rate of 0.3 would allow 0.7 to survive from the 0.9 that normally survive, for an effective survival rate of $(0.7)(0.9)$ or 0.63. Multiplying the survival rates in the Leslie matrix by $1 - h$ will model uniform harvesting in the existing population. In addition, we must also consider the newborn population. Newborn animals are added during a cycle according to the birth rates; however, birth rates are normally multiplied with the existing, unharvested population. To account for harvesting of the existing population, the birth rates must also be multiplied by a factor of $1 - h$. For example, suppose an age group of a population has a birth rate of 0.8, and 0.3 of the animals are harvested during each cycle. After harvesting, only 0.7 of the females in this group will actually be available for giving birth. The birth rate for the 0.7 of the animals left after harvesting is still 0.8, but the effective birth rate for this group that accounts for harvesting is $(0.8)(0.7)$ or 0.56. So we see that uniform harvesting by a factor of h is accomplished by multiplying the survival rates and the birth rates by $1 - h$.

Adjusting the Leslie matrix L by multiplying survival rates and birth rates by $1 - h$ is easily done by multiplying the matrix L by the scalar $1 - h$. The new Leslie matrix L' that includes uniform harvesting is given by the equation

$$L' = (1 - h)L.$$

In section 5.2, we observed that a population modeled with the Leslie matrix eventually grows at a constant percentage rate, which we call r. What is the effect of uniform harvesting on the long-term growth rate?

Without harvesting, the age distribution vector X_k satisfies the equation

$$X_k = (1 + r)X_{k-1}$$

for large k. By large k we mean values of k large enough that the stable growth pattern for the population has been reached. We also know that the original model (without harvesting) is based on the relationship

$$X_k = LX_{k-1}.$$

Comparing the two preceding equations shows that for large k, multiplication by L effectively multiplies X_{k-1} by a factor of $1 + r$.

Suppose that at some point in the process harvesting begins, and a new Leslie matrix L' is introduced to generate the age distribution vectors. If harvesting starts immediately during the first cycle, then the original matrix L is never used and L' takes over from the beginning. If harvesting begins during the tenth cycle, then L is used to find the first nine vectors and L' is used for succeeding vectors from cycle 10 onward.

When a uniform harvesting factor is introduced and L is replaced by $L' = (1 - h)L$, then the new age distribution vector X_k is found from the relationship

$$X_k = L'X_{k-1}.$$

Substituting for L' in terms of L, the equation

$$X_k = (1 - h)LX_{k-1}$$

is satisfied for each cycle after harvesting begins. With the original matrix L, X_{k-1} is multiplied by $1 + r$, which implies that after harvesting begins,

$$X_k = (1 - h)(1 + r)X_{k-1}.$$

The equation above reveals that L' effectively multiplies the populations of the separate age groups by $(1 - h)(1 + r)$ in the long run.

Let P_k be the total female population after k cycles. P_k is a single value, not a matrix of values like X_k. The value of P_k is determined by summing the entries in X_k. In section 5.2, we found that the long-term growth rate of the entire population is the same as the long-term growth rate of each age group. Without harvesting, therefore, the total female population P_k satisfies the equation

$$P_k = (1 + r)P_{k-1}$$

for large k. Likewise, the total female population with harvesting grows according to the equation

$$P_k = (1 - h)(1 + r)P_{k-1}.$$

Referring to the equations for X_k and P_k, we observe that the long-term effect of uniform harvesting is to change the multiplying factor for the total population and the age distribution vectors from $1 + r$ to $(1 - h)(1 + r)$.

We are now able to solve the problem of determining a uniform harvesting rate that will yield zero population growth. The objective of harvesting is to have $P_k = P_{k-1}$ after a certain number of cycles. Since uniform harvesting leads to the long-term relationship $P_k = (1 - h)(1 + r)P_{k-1}$, we want to choose h so that

$$(1 - h)(1 + r) = 1.$$

Solving for h, we find that

$$1 - h = \frac{1}{1 + r},$$

so that

$$h = 1 - \frac{1}{1 + r}.$$

The new Leslie matrix L' that includes uniform harvesting to achieve a stable population is related to the original Leslie matrix L by $L' = (1 - h)L$, or, in terms of r,

$$L' = \frac{1}{1 + r}L.$$

Example: What harvesting strategy should be used to achieve a stable population of about 200 in the woodland mammal example using the initial age distribution of the population shown in Table 3 on page 35?

Before discussing a harvesting strategy, we must first determine when the total population is 200. The Leslie matrix models the female population, so we need to know when the female population reaches 100. In Section 5.2, we found that the total female population after 10 cycles is about 63 and the long-term growth rate of the population is 3.04%. The multiplying factor for the population is 1.0304, so we can find approximately how many cycles t are required to go from 63 to 100 females by solving the exponential equation

$$100 = 63(1.0304)^t.$$

Using logarithms we find that

$$t = \frac{\ln(100/63)}{\ln 1.0304}$$

or

$$t \approx 15.43.$$

About 10 cycles are required to reach a population of 63, and about another 15 or 16 cycles to grow from 63 to 100. We expect, therefore, that a total of 25 or 26 cycles are required for the female population to reach 100. In fact, calculations reveal that the total female population is about 98 after 25 cycles, and about 101 after 26 cycles.

The harvesting factor h that will achieve zero population growth is

$$
\begin{aligned}
h &= 1 - \frac{1}{1+r} \\
&= 1 - \frac{1}{1+0.0304} \\
&= 0.0295.
\end{aligned}
$$

The harvesting strategy that will result in a stable population of about 100 females is as follows:

1. Wait 26 cycles, or 78 months, until the female population reaches about 100 and the total population reaches about 200.

2. After 78 months, remove 2.95% of the mammals uniformly from each age group during every 3-month cycle, which also removes 2.95% of the females uniformly from each age group.

A harvesting factor of $h = 0.0295$ is incorporated into the Leslie matrix model by multiplying the original Leslie matrix by the factor $1 - h = 0.9705$. Note that the quantity $1 - h$ can be calculated directly without first finding h by using the equation

$$
\begin{aligned}
1 - h &= \frac{1}{1+r} \\
&= \frac{1}{1+0.0304} \\
&= 0.9705.
\end{aligned}
$$

Calculations with the new Leslie matrix $L' = 0.9705L$ operating on the age distribution vector X_{26} confirms that the total female population remains stable at about 101.

The numbers in this example may seem strange. After all, how can we harvest 2.95% of each of 6 age groups in a total population of only 100 females? We would remove less than one animal from each age group every 3 months. This happens because the numbers in this example are deliberately small for the sake of simplicity. Suppose, however, that the units of the population are in thousands for a total female population of 100,000. For this larger population, the strategy for harvesting is the same, and the numbers are more realistic.

■

When the Leslie matrix model is applied to the problem of stabilizing the growth of certain populations, another strategy focuses on reducing the birth rate. Assuming the birth rates for all age groups are reduced by the same proportion, how much should birth rates be reduced to achieve zero population growth?

To answer this question, we need to calculate a quantity R called the *net reproduction rate*. R is defined as the expected number of female offspring for a female during her entire lifetime. A formula for R can be derived in terms of the birth rates B_k and survival rates S_k for the k different age groups, with $k = 1, 2, \ldots, n$. During her time in the first age group, a female would expect to have B_1 female offspring. During her time in the second age group, she would expect to have B_2 female offspring; however, her chance of surviving to the second age group is S_1. Her expected number of female offspring during the first two age groups would thus be $B_1 + B_2 S_1$. Her expected number of female offspring in the third age group is B_3, but her chance of surviving to the third age group is $S_1 S_2$. During the first three age groups, we find that a female's expected number of female offspring is $B_1 + B_2 S_1 + B_3 S_1 S_2$. Continuing this reasoning throughout the n age groups of a female's lifetime, the expected number of female offspring during a female's entire lifetime is

$$R = B_1 + B_2 S_1 + B_3 S_1 S_2 + \cdots + B_n S_1 S_2 \cdots S_{n-1}.$$

To achieve zero population growth, the net reproduction rate R needs to be reduced to 1. Each term in the formula for R includes a birth rate for a different age group; therefore, reducing each birth rate by the same proportion b will have the effect of reducing R by the proportion b. To reduce the birth rates by 10%, we multiply each B_k by 0.9, which in turn multiplies R by 0.9. To reduce the birth rates by a factor b, multiply each B_k by $1 - b$, which also multiplies R by $1 - b$. Reducing each birth rate by a factor b thus yields a new net reproduction rate R' such that

$$R' = (1 - b)R.$$

Zero population growth is achieved by choosing b so that $R' = 1$. Substitution for R' yields

$$(1 - b)R = 1,$$

or, equivalently,

$$1 - b = \frac{1}{R}.$$

Choosing $1 - b$ as the reciprocal of R effectively reduces the net reproduction rate to 1. Solving for b, we have

$$b = 1 - \frac{1}{R}.$$

If $R = 2$, then we would choose $b = 1/2$, which cuts the birth rates in half. If $R = 3$, then we would choose $b = 2/3$; therefore, we would seek to reduce the birth rates by a factor of $2/3$, which is equivalent to multiplying the birth rates by $1/3$. If $R = 1.5$, then we would choose $b = 1/3$, which implies reducing the birth rates by $1/3$ or multiplying the birth rates by $2/3$.

The reduced birth rates are incorporated into a new Leslie matrix either (a) by introducing a new Leslie matrix with the original survival rates and the new birth rates or (b) by left-multiplying the original $n \times n$ Leslie matrix by the $n \times n$ matrix

$$\begin{pmatrix} 1-b & 0 & 0 & \cdots & 0 \\ 0 & 1 & 0 & \cdots & 0 \\ 0 & 0 & 1 & \cdots & 0 \\ \vdots & \vdots & \vdots & \vdots & \vdots \\ 0 & 0 & 0 & \cdots & 1 \end{pmatrix}.$$

The matrix above is an identity matrix except that the entry in row 1, column 1 is changed from 1 to $1 - b$. Left-multiplying the original Leslie matrix by this matrix will multiply the first row by $1 - b$ and leave the other rows unchanged. As a result, the birth rates will be multiplied by $1 - b$ and the survival rates will remain the same.

5.5   Exercises

1. Refer to the animal population with the birth rates, death rates, and initial age distribution given in Exercise 6 of section 5.3.

   (a) What uniform harvesting strategy can be used to stabilize the population at its maximum of 700?

   (b) Construct the new Leslie matrix that incorporates your strategy of part (a). Verify that this strategy will indeed stabilize the population at 700.

2. The 1965 birth rates and survival rates for Canadian women less than 50 years old and a sample initial female population distribution are given in the table shown below. (See H. Anton and C. Rorres, *Elementary Linear Algebra with Applications*, John Wiley and Sons (New York), 1987, p. 634.)

Age interval	Birth rate	Survival rate	Initial pop.
$[0, 5)$	0.00000	0.99651	100,000
$[5, 10)$	0.00024	0.99820	90,000
$[10, 15)$	0.05861	0.99802	85,000
$[15, 20)$	0.28608	0.99729	79,000
$[20, 25)$	0.44791	0.99694	72,000
$[25, 30)$	0.36399	0.99621	65,000
$[30, 35)$	0.22259	0.99460	60,000
$[35, 40)$	0.10457	0.99184	58,000
$[40, 45)$	0.02826	0.98700	53,000
$[45, 50)$	0.00240	—	50,000

(a) What is the long-term growth rate of the Canadian population under 50 years old if Canadian women continue to reproduce and die at the same rates as in 1965?

(b) By how much must the birth rates be reduced to achieve zero population growth?

(c) Based on the 1965 data, construct a new Leslie matrix that includes birth rates adjusted for zero population growth, and verify that this model achieves the desired results.

3. A certain species of domestic sheep in New Zealand has a life span of 12 years. Dividing the sheep into 12 age classes of one year each, the following birth rates and survival rates were found (see G. Caughley, "Parameters for Seasonally Breeding Populations," *Ecology*, 1967, pp. 834–839):

Age	Birth rate	Survival rate
0–1	0.000	0.845
1–2	0.045	0.975
2–3	0.391	0.965
3–4	0.472	0.950
4–5	0.484	0.926
5–6	0.546	0.896
6–7	0.543	0.850
7–8	0.502	0.786
8–9	0.468	0.691
9–10	0.459	0.561
10–11	0.433	0.370
11–12	0.421	0.000

(a) What is the long-term growth rate of the sheep population?

(b) What uniform harvesting policy will stabilize the sheep population?

(c) After implementing the uniform harvesting policy determined in part (b), what percentage of the total sheep population will be found in each of the 12 age groups?

6 Markov Chains

This section begins with an example that illustrates many of the essential features of constructing a class of matrix models called Markov chains.

Example 1—The Taxi Problem: A taxi company has divided the city into 3 regions—Northside, Downtown, and Southside. By keeping track of pickups and deliveries, the company has found that of the fares picked up in Northside, 50% stay in that region, 20% are taken Downtown, and 30% go to Southside. Of the fares picked up Downtown, only 10% go to Northside, 40% stay Downtown, and 50% go to Southside. Of the fares picked up in Southside, 30% go to each of Northside and Downtown, while 40% stay in Southside.

We would like to know what the distribution of taxis will be over time as they pick up and drop off successive fares. This is a difficult analysis that we will approach first through a simpler question in this example. Examples later in this section will gradually work toward the analysis of the long-term distribution of taxis throughout the city. The question we will examine for now is the following: If a taxi starts off Downtown, what is the probability that it will be Downtown after letting off its third fare?

The information in this example can be represented with a state diagram which includes (a) three states D, N, and S corresponding to the three regions of the city; and (b) the probabilities of moving from one region to another. The state diagram for the Taxi Problem is shown in Figure 8. In general, the movement from one state to another is called a *transition*. In this example, a transition corresponds to a customer being picked up in a region and dropped off in a region. Transitions to all three regions are feasible from every region; therefore, each state in the state diagram is connected to all other states, including itself.

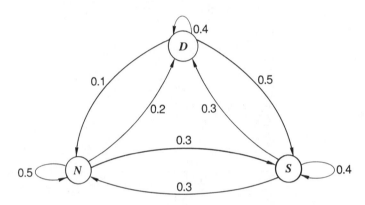

Figure 8: State Diagram for the Taxi Problem

A taxi that starts off Downtown and ends up Downtown after 3 fares can follow several different paths through the state diagram. It could go Southside after 1 fare, then Northside after 2 fares, and end up Downtown after 3 fares; or, it could go Northside, Downtown, and Downtown on its 3 fares. This reasoning shows that we must consider all possible combinations of fares such that the third fare ends up Downtown. The picture in Figure 9, called a *tree diagram*, shows all possible paths starting Downtown and picking up three fares, with the third fare ending up Downtown. With a taxi picking up a fare Downtown, there is a probability of 0.10 that the taxi will go to Northside, a probability of 0.40 of dropping off the fare Downtown, and a probability of 0.50 of heading to Southside. These probabilities are indicated in the tree diagram on the lines, called *branches*, that represent the possible destinations of the first fare. The first set of branches start at D and end at N, D, and S. The branches representing the second fare likewise have the associated probabilities shown in the tree diagram. Each path through the tree from the starting D to the ending D represents a possible sequence of three fares in which the first fare starts Downtown and the third fare ends Downtown. Every such path has a probability of occurring that is determined by multiplying the probabilities for each branch in the path. Our objective is to determine the probabilities associated with following each of the possible paths through the tree diagram.

After 1 fare, the probabilities of being Northside (N), Downtown (D), and Southside (S) are

$$P(N_1) = 0.1, \quad P(D_1) = 0.4, \quad \text{and} \quad P(S_1) = 0.5,$$

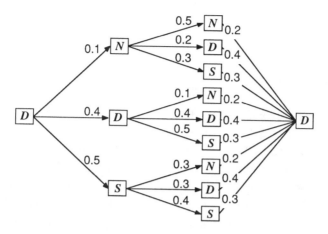

Figure 9: Tree Diagram for the Taxi Problem

where the subscripts refer to the number of fares.

Referring to the tree diagram, we observe that after 2 fares, the probability of being Northside can be expressed in symbols as

$$P(N_2) = P(N_1)P(NN) + P(D_1)P(DN) + P(S_1)P(SN),$$

where $P(NN)$ is the probability of going from Northside to Northside, $P(DN)$ is the probability of going from Downtown to Northside, and $P(SN)$ is the probability of going from Southside to Northside. Likewise, the probabilities of being Downtown and Southside after 2 fares are

$$P(D_2) = P(N_1)P(ND) + P(D_1)P(DD) + P(S_1)P(SD)$$

and

$$P(S_2) = P(N_1)P(NS) + P(D_1)P(DS) + P(S_1)P(SS).$$

Each of the terms in the sums above is a product of two probabilities—of being in a certain first region after one fare and of going from the first to the second region on the second fare. For example, $P(N_1)P(NS)$ is the probability of going to Northside on the first fare times the probability of going from Northside to Southside on the second fare. Substituting the appropriate values from the tree diagram in the sums gives the following:

$$P(N_2) = (0.1)(0.5) + (0.4)(0.1) + (0.5)(0.3) = 0.24$$

$$P(D_2) = (0.1)(0.2) + (0.4)(0.4) + (0.5)(0.3) = 0.33$$

$$P(S_2) = (0.1)(0.3) + (0.4)(0.5) + (0.5)(0.4) = 0.43$$

Notice that $P(N_2) + P(D_2) + P(S_2) = 1$, meaning that the taxi must be in one of the 3 regions after 2 fares, as expected.

The probability of being Downtown after 3 fares is

$$\begin{aligned} P(D_3) &= P(N_2)P(ND) + P(D_2)P(DD) + P(S_2)P(SD) \\ &= (0.24)(0.2) + (0.33)(0.4) + (0.43)(0.3) \\ &= 0.309. \end{aligned}$$

A taxi starting Downtown has a probability of 0.309 of being Downtown after 3 fares.

∎

The preceding example describes mathematical modeling techniques for analyzing the behavior of a system that includes a finite number of states—the three regions of the city—and probabilities of transitions from each state to every other possible state. We assume that a transition—picking up and dropping off a fare—occurs each time the system is observed, and that observations occur at regular intervals. Systems with these characteristics are called *Markov chains* or *Markov processes*.

Suppose we wish to take the Taxi Problem further and determine the probability of a taxi being Downtown after five fares if it started Downtown. At this point, finding the probability of being Downtown after five fares appears to be a tedious endeavor. Let us return to the calculations we used to determine the probability of being Downtown after three fares. From our previous experiences with matrices, we might guess that the calculations above can be simplified considerably with the use of matrix multiplication. The probabilities of being in each region after two fares, represented by $P(N_2)$, $P(D_2)$, and $P(S_2)$, were calculated by finding sums of products. The first product in each sum has a factor of 0.1; the second product in each sum has a factor of 0.4; and the third product in each sum has a factor of 0.5. These observations lead us to deduce that the probabilities of being in each region after two fares are given by the row vector resulting from the matrix multiplication shown below:

$$\begin{pmatrix} 0.1 & 0.4 & 0.5 \end{pmatrix} \begin{pmatrix} 0.5 & 0.2 & 0.3 \\ 0.1 & 0.4 & 0.5 \\ 0.3 & 0.3 & 0.4 \end{pmatrix} = \begin{pmatrix} 0.24 & 0.33 & 0.43 \end{pmatrix}$$

The matrix T defined by

$$T = \begin{matrix} & \begin{matrix} N & D & S \end{matrix} \\ \begin{matrix} N \\ D \\ S \end{matrix} & \begin{pmatrix} 0.5 & 0.2 & 0.3 \\ 0.1 & 0.4 & 0.5 \\ 0.3 & 0.3 & 0.4 \end{pmatrix} \end{matrix}$$

is crucial to our calculations. T is called a *transition matrix* because it contains entries such that T_{ij} is the probability of a transition from region i to region j. For example, T_{13} is the probability of a fare that originates in Northside going to Southside. The probability of a fare that originates in Southside going to Downtown is T_{32}. Continuing with our analysis of the previous calculations, observe that the probability of being Downtown after three fares is equal to the product of the row vector after two fares and the column vector composing the second column of T, as shown below:

$$\begin{pmatrix} 0.24 & 0.33 & 0.43 \end{pmatrix} \begin{pmatrix} 0.2 \\ 0.4 \\ 0.3 \end{pmatrix} = 0.309$$

Substitution of the matrix product that produced the leftmost matrix in the equation above yields

$$\begin{pmatrix} 0.1 & 0.4 & 0.5 \end{pmatrix} \begin{pmatrix} 0.5 & 0.2 & 0.3 \\ 0.1 & 0.4 & 0.5 \\ 0.3 & 0.3 & 0.4 \end{pmatrix} \begin{pmatrix} 0.2 \\ 0.4 \\ 0.3 \end{pmatrix} = 0.309$$

Instead of using only the second column of T as the rightmost matrix in the product above, substitute the entire matrix T as follows:

$$\begin{pmatrix} 0.1 & 0.4 & 0.5 \end{pmatrix} \begin{pmatrix} 0.5 & 0.2 & 0.3 \\ 0.1 & 0.4 & 0.5 \\ 0.3 & 0.3 & 0.4 \end{pmatrix} \begin{pmatrix} 0.5 & 0.2 & 0.3 \\ 0.1 & 0.4 & 0.5 \\ 0.3 & 0.3 & 0.4 \end{pmatrix} = \begin{pmatrix} 0.282 & 0.309 & 0.409 \end{pmatrix}$$

The leftmost matrix above is merely the second row of T. It can be found by left-multiplying T by the vector (0 1 0); therefore, the calculations through three fares can be written as

$$\begin{pmatrix} 0 & 1 & 0 \end{pmatrix} \begin{pmatrix} 0.5 & 0.2 & 0.3 \\ 0.1 & 0.4 & 0.5 \\ 0.3 & 0.3 & 0.4 \end{pmatrix} \begin{pmatrix} 0.5 & 0.2 & 0.3 \\ 0.1 & 0.4 & 0.5 \\ 0.3 & 0.3 & 0.4 \end{pmatrix} \begin{pmatrix} 0.5 & 0.2 & 0.3 \\ 0.1 & 0.4 & 0.5 \\ 0.3 & 0.3 & 0.4 \end{pmatrix},$$

which is equivalent to

$$\begin{pmatrix} 0 & 1 & 0 \end{pmatrix} T^3 = \begin{pmatrix} 0.282 & 0.309 & 0.409 \end{pmatrix}.$$

The probability of being Downtown after three fares when starting out Downtown is 0.309, the middle entry in the row vector shown above. What is the meaning of the other entries in this row vector? The result of multiplying T^3 by (0 1 0) is the second row of T^3, specifically (0.282 0.309 0.409). Rather than focus only on the second row of T^3, let us examine the following more general question: What meaning should we attach to all of the entries of T^3?

Before answering this question, consider the entries in T^2 shown below.

$$T^2 = \begin{array}{c} N \\ D \\ S \end{array} \begin{array}{ccc} N & D & S \\ \begin{pmatrix} 0.5 & 0.2 & 0.3 \\ 0.1 & 0.4 & 0.5 \\ 0.3 & 0.3 & 0.4 \end{pmatrix} \end{array} \begin{array}{c} N \\ D \\ S \end{array} \begin{array}{ccc} N & D & S \\ \begin{pmatrix} 0.5 & 0.2 & 0.3 \\ 0.1 & 0.4 & 0.5 \\ 0.3 & 0.3 & 0.4 \end{pmatrix} \end{array} = \begin{array}{c} N \\ D \\ S \end{array} \begin{array}{ccc} N & D & S \\ \begin{pmatrix} 0.36 & 0.27 & 0.37 \\ 0.24 & 0.33 & 0.43 \\ 0.3 & 0.3 & 0.4 \end{pmatrix} \end{array}$$

The entry in row 1, column 2 of T^2 is derived by multiplying row 1 of T by column 2 of T as follows:

$$(0.5)(0.2) + (0.2)(0.4) + (0.3)(0.3) = 0.27.$$

Row 1 of T contains the probabilities for the transitions from N to each of the regions, whereas column 2 of T contains the probabilities for the transitions from each of the regions to D. In symbols, the product of row 1 times column 2 is

$$P(NN)P(ND) + P(ND)P(DD) + P(NS)P(SD),$$

which is the probability of going from region N to region D after 2 transitions. In the matrix T^2, the entry in row 1, column 2 has row label N and column label D, and it represents the probability of going from N to D in 2 transitions. Using similar reasoning, it can be shown that the entry in row 1, column 1 of T^2 gives the probability of starting in N and ending in N after 2 transitions. In general, the ij entry of T^2 gives the probability of starting in region i and ending in region j after 2 transitions.

What about the entries in T^3 shown below?

$$T^3 = \begin{array}{c} \\ N \\ D \\ S \end{array} \begin{array}{ccc} N & D & S \\ \left(\begin{array}{ccc} 0.318 & 0.291 & 0.391 \\ 0.282 & 0.309 & 0.409 \\ 0.3 & 0.3 & 0.4 \end{array} \right) \end{array}$$

The row and column labels were useful in interpreting T^2, and they are included with T^3 as well. The probability of being in region D three transitions after starting in region D, which we found to be 0.309, is the entry with row label D and column label D. By reasoning similar to that used with T^2, we can deduce that the entry in row D, column S is the probability of ending in region S three transitions after starting in region D. In general, entry ij of T^3 gives the probability of starting in region i and ending in region j after 3 transitions.

We now return to the question under consideration: If a taxi starts off Downtown, what is the probability that it will be Downtown after letting off its 5th fare? The answer to this question is found in the entry in row D and column D of T^5, which is 0.30081, as shown in the matrix below calculated with computer software.

$$T^5 = \begin{array}{c} \\ N \\ D \\ S \end{array} \begin{array}{ccc} N & D & S \\ \left(\begin{array}{ccc} 0.30162 & 0.29919 & 0.39919 \\ 0.29838 & 0.30081 & 0.40081 \\ 0.3 & 0.3 & 0.4 \end{array} \right) \end{array}$$

Example 2: In the Taxi Problem, where should a taxi start to have the best chance of being Northside after 3 fares?

The probability of being in each region for each possible starting region is given by the matrix T^3 shown below.

$$T^3 = \begin{array}{c} \\ N \\ D \\ S \end{array} \begin{array}{ccc} N & D & S \\ \left(\begin{array}{ccc} 0.318 & 0.291 & 0.391 \\ 0.282 & 0.309 & 0.409 \\ 0.3 & 0.3 & 0.4 \end{array} \right) \end{array}$$

The probability of ending up in Northside for each starting place is found in column 1, the N column, of T^3. The Northside entry is the largest in this column, so starting in Northside offers the best chance of being Northside after 3 fares—a probability of 0.318.

■

On the basis of the work in the first two examples, the following general observations can be made about a transition matrix T for a Markov chain:

1. *A transition matrix is square.* This characteristic is obvious because the number of rows and the number of columns are both the same as the number of states.

2. *All entries are between 0 and 1 inclusive.* This follows from the fact that the entries correspond to transition probabilities from one state to another.

3. *The sum of the entries in any row must be 1.* The sum of the entries in an entire row is the sum of the transition probabilities from one state to all other states. Since a transition is sure to take place, this sum must be 1.

4. *The ij entry in the matrix T^n gives the probability of being in state j after n transitions, with state i as the initial state.*

5. *The entries in the transition matrix are constant.* A Markov chain model depends upon the assumption that the transition matrix does not change throughout the process. This implies that to determine the state of the system after any transition, it is necessary to know only the immediately preceding state of the system. Knowledge of the prior behavior of the system is not needed provided that the immediately preceding state is known.

Example 3: A bag contains 3 red and 4 green jelly beans. Suppose you take out 3 beans, one at a time, and eat them. What is the probability that the third bean chosen is green?

This problem is an example of a probabilistic situation in which all of the previous behavior of the system must be examined; therefore, it is not modeled as a Markov chain. The set of beans chosen in all previous selections will affect the probability of choosing each color in the present selection. The outcomes that have a green jelly bean chosen third are RRG, RGG, GRG, and GGG, where R stands for choosing a red jelly bean and G stands for choosing a green jelly bean. Taking into account the beans remaining after each selection, each outcome has the probabilities listed below.

$$P(RRG) = \left(\frac{3}{7}\right)\left(\frac{2}{6}\right)\left(\frac{4}{5}\right) \quad P(RGG) = \left(\frac{3}{7}\right)\left(\frac{4}{6}\right)\left(\frac{3}{5}\right)$$

$$P(GRG) = \left(\frac{4}{7}\right)\left(\frac{3}{6}\right)\left(\frac{3}{5}\right) \quad P(GGG) = \left(\frac{4}{7}\right)\left(\frac{3}{6}\right)\left(\frac{2}{5}\right)$$

The answer to this problem is the sum of the 4 products above, which is

$$\frac{24 + 36 + 36 + 24}{7 \cdot 6 \cdot 5} = \frac{120}{210} = \frac{4}{7}.$$

The probability that the third jelly bean drawn from the bag is green is 4/7.

∎

The problem in Example 3 is a simple example of a *stochastic process.* In a generalized stochastic process, the transition probabilities are not necessarily constant or independent of the previous behavior of the system. Notice that in Example 3, the probability of drawing a red jelly bean will vary depending on the number of beans of each color that have been chosen previously. A Markov chain is a special case of a stochastic process in which the transition probabilities are constant and independent of the previous behavior of the system. In a Markov chain, the next state is determined solely by the unchanging transition probabilities and the current state of the system. The route that is followed to arrive at the current state does not affect the transition matrix; only the current state of the system is relevant.

Example 4: In the Taxi Problem, the cab company initially places 25% of the cars Northside, 40% of the cars Downtown, and 35% of the cars Southside. What will be the distribution of cars after each has made 3 pickups?

Represent the initial distribution of cars with the row vector

$$X_0 = \begin{pmatrix} N & D & S \\ 0.25 & 0.40 & 0.35 \end{pmatrix}.$$

To find the percentage of cars Northside after one pickup, multiply the percentage of the cars in each region by the probability of going from that region to Northside and add the resulting products:

$$(0.25)(0.5) + (0.40)(0.1) + (0.35)(0.3) = 0.27$$

This sum is just the product of X_0 and the first column of the transition matrix T. Likewise, the percentage of cars Downtown after one pickup is equal to the product of X_0 and the second column, the D column, of T. The percentage of cars Southside after one pickup is equal to the product of X_0 and the third column of T. The distribution X_1 of cars after one pickup is therefore given by

$$X_1 = X_0 T$$

$$= \begin{pmatrix} N & D & S \\ 0.25 & 0.40 & 0.35 \end{pmatrix} \begin{array}{c} N \\ D \\ S \end{array} \begin{pmatrix} N & D & S \\ 0.5 & 0.2 & 0.3 \\ 0.1 & 0.4 & 0.5 \\ 0.3 & 0.3 & 0.4 \end{pmatrix}$$

$$= \begin{pmatrix} N & D & S \\ 0.27 & 0.315 & 0.415 \end{pmatrix}.$$

Continuing this line of reasoning, we see that X_2, the distribution of cars after 2 fares, is given by

$$X_2 = X_1 T$$
$$= X_0 T^2.$$

The distribution of cars after 3 pickups is

$$X_3 = X_2 T$$
$$= X_0 T^3,$$

which is

$$X_3 = \begin{pmatrix} N & D & S \\ 0.25 & 0.40 & 0.35 \end{pmatrix} \begin{array}{c} N \\ D \\ S \end{array} \begin{pmatrix} N & D & S \\ 0.318 & 0.291 & 0.391 \\ 0.282 & 0.309 & 0.409 \\ 0.3 & 0.3 & 0.4 \end{pmatrix}$$

$$= \begin{pmatrix} N & D & S \\ 0.2973 & 0.30135 & 0.40135 \end{pmatrix}.$$

After 3 fares, about 30% of the taxis are Northside, about 30% are Downtown, and about 40% are Southside.

∎

The vector $X_k = X_0 T^k$ is called the *state vector* for a Markov chain after k transitions with an initial distribution X_0. The jth entry of X_k is the probability of being in state j after k transitions.

Example 5: For the Taxi Problem with the initial state vector given in Example 4, what is the long-term distribution of cars?

We found X_3 in Example 4. After 5 pickups, we have

$$
\begin{array}{c}
N \quad\; D \quad\;\; S \\
X_5 = \begin{pmatrix} 0.25 & 0.40 & 0.35 \end{pmatrix} T^5 \\[4pt]
\; N \qquad\;\; D \qquad\;\; S \\
= \begin{pmatrix} 0.299757 & 0.300121 & 0.400121 \end{pmatrix}.
\end{array}
$$

Moving along even further, the state vector after 10 pickups is

$$
\begin{array}{c}
X_{10} = X_0 T^{10} \\[4pt]
\phantom{X_{10} =}\; N \qquad\; D \quad\;\; S \\
= \begin{pmatrix} 0.299999 & 0.3 & 0.4 \end{pmatrix},
\end{array}
$$

and after 15 pickups,

$$
\begin{array}{c}
X_{15} = X_0 T^{15} \\[4pt]
\phantom{X_{15} =}\; N \quad\; D \quad\; S \\
= \begin{pmatrix} 0.3 & 0.3 & 0.4 \end{pmatrix}.
\end{array}
$$

A trend is clear in the state vector X_k—it converges to the vector $\begin{pmatrix} 0.3 & 0.3 & 0.4 \end{pmatrix}$. Further transitions after the 15th pickup will not change this distribution.

∎

Evidently, the system represented by the Markov process in the Taxi Problem stabilizes; that is, after a certain number of transitions the distribution of taxis is not changed by additional transitions. In other words, the state vector eventually reaches a stable distribution even after repeated multiplication by the transition matrix. In symbols, stability means that for large enough k, we find that $X_k T = X_k$. From another point of view, since $X_{k+1} = X_k T$, we eventually reach a point beyond which $X_k = X_{k+1}$. This is called the *stable state*. The *stable state vector* of a Markov process is a vector X such that $X = XT$, where T is the transition matrix. The entries in the stable state vector were found in Example 5 by multiplying by T a large number of times, calculations made easy by the use of computer software.

Class Practice

1. Let the following matrix represent a transition matrix for a Markov chain.

$$T = \begin{array}{c} \\ 1 \\ 2 \\ 3 \end{array} \begin{array}{ccc} 1 & 2 & 3 \\ \begin{pmatrix} 0.2 & 0.4 & 0.4 \\ 0.4 & 0.2 & 0.4 \\ 0 & 0.3 & 0.7 \end{pmatrix} \end{array}$$

(a) What is the probability of moving from state 1 to state 3? From state 3 to state 1?

(b) If the system is in state 2, what is the probability of staying there on the next transition?

2. What is the stable state vector of the Taxi Problem? Does the stable state vector depend upon the initial distribution? What does changing the initial distribution have to do with reaching a stable state?

We have examined the behavior of the distribution X_k for a particular initial distribution X_0. As X_k approaches the stable state vector, what is happening to the entries of T^k? The calculation of T^5, T^{10}, and T^{15}, shown below, reveals that each row of T^k converges to the stable state vector.

$$T^5 = \begin{array}{c} \\ N \\ D \\ S \end{array} \begin{array}{ccc} N & D & S \\ \begin{pmatrix} 0.30162 & 0.29919 & 0.39919 \\ 0.29838 & 0.30081 & 0.40081 \\ 0.3 & 0.3 & 0.4 \end{pmatrix} \end{array}$$

$$T^{10} = \begin{array}{c} \\ N \\ D \\ S \end{array} \begin{array}{ccc} N & D & S \\ \begin{pmatrix} 0.300004 & 0.299998 & 0.399998 \\ 0.299996 & 0.300002 & 0.400002 \\ 0.3 & 0.3 & 0.4 \end{pmatrix} \end{array}$$

$$T^{15} = \begin{array}{c} \\ N \\ D \\ S \end{array} \begin{array}{ccc} N & D & S \\ \begin{pmatrix} 0.3 & 0.3 & 0.4 \\ 0.3 & 0.3 & 0.4 \\ 0.3 & 0.3 & 0.4 \end{pmatrix} \end{array}$$

What is the implication of this phenomenon? Recall that row i of T^k contains the probabilities of ending in each state after k transitions from a starting state i. Since each row converges to the stable state vector, we can infer that the stable state vector is independent of the starting state. No matter what initial distribution is specified, the state vector will converge to the same stable state vector, which is equal to each row of T^k for large k. Care must be taken, however, when T is raised to a large power using computer software. Round-off errors could actually cause T^k to diverge for sufficiently large k. One strategy for dealing with the effects of round-off errors is to examine the behavior of T^k at various points in the process, and not just at one large value of k.

Not all Markov chains have a stable state vector. Consider the transition matrix A shown below.

$$A = \begin{pmatrix} 0.3 & 0.1 & 0.4 & 0 & 0.2 \\ 0 & 1 & 0 & 0 & 0 \\ 0.2 & 0.3 & 0.1 & 0.1 & 0.3 \\ 0 & 0 & 0 & 1 & 0 \\ 0.2 & 0.2 & 0.1 & 0.5 & 0 \end{pmatrix}$$

For large powers of k, we find that A^k converges to

$$\begin{pmatrix} 0 & 0.587097 & 0 & 0.412903 & 0 \\ 0 & 1 & 0 & 0 & 0 \\ 0 & 0.589247 & 0 & 0.410753 & 0 \\ 0 & 0 & 0 & 1 & 0 \\ 0 & 0.376344 & 0 & 0.623656 & 0 \end{pmatrix}.$$

The diversity of the rows of A^k for large k assures us that no stable state vector exists for this system. The probability of ending in a certain state after stability is reached clearly depends on the starting state.

Observe that in transition matrix A, once the system enters state 2 or state 4, it can never leave that state. Zeros in rows 2 and 4 indicate a probability of zero that the system will change to another state once it is in state 2 or state 4. These states are called *absorbing states*. The row corresponding to an absorbing state contains a 1 on the diagonal of the matrix and 0s for all of the other entries. An *absorbing-state Markov chain* is a Markov chain such that (a) it has at least one absorbing state and (b) it is possible to move from any nonabsorbing state to an absorbing state. A process modeled with an absorbing-state Markov chain will eventually end up in one of the absorbing states, as can be observed with matrix A above. The only nonzero entries in a large power of A are found in the absorbing-state columns.

How do we know if a Markov chain has a stable state vector? A sufficient condition, which is stated without proof, for a Markov chain to have a stable state vector is that some power of the transition matrix has only nonzero entries. A Markov chain satisfying this criterion is called *regular*. For example, a Markov chain with transition matrix

$$B = \begin{pmatrix} 0.2 & 0.8 \\ 1 & 0 \end{pmatrix}$$

is regular since

$$B^2 = \begin{pmatrix} 0.84 & 0.16 \\ 0.2 & 0.8 \end{pmatrix}.$$

For regular Markov chains, we can find the stable state vector by raising the transition matrix to a large power. As the power increases, the rows of the transition matrix each approach the stable state vector. A stable state vector may not exist in an absorbing-state Markov chain; however, the transition matrix raised to a large power may have rows that converge to some vector, but not necessarily the same vector for each row.

6.1 Exercises

1. A rat is placed in the maze shown in Figure 10. During a fixed time interval, the rat randomly chooses one of the doors available to it (depending upon which room it is in) and moves through that door to the next room—it does not remain in the room it occupies. Each movement of the rat is taken as a transition in a Markov chain in which a state is identified with the room the rat is in. The first row of the transition matrix is

$$\begin{array}{ccccc} 1 & 2 & 3 & 4 & 5 \end{array}$$
$$1 \begin{pmatrix} 0 & \frac{1}{2} & 0 & 0 & \frac{1}{2} \end{pmatrix}.$$

   (a) Construct the entire transition matrix for this process.

   (b) If the rat starts in room 1, what is the probability that it is in room 3 after two transitions? After three transitions?

   (c) Determine the stable state vector.

   (d) After a large number of transitions, what is the probability that the rat is in room 4?

   (e) In the long run, what percentage of the time will the rat spend in rooms 2 or 3?

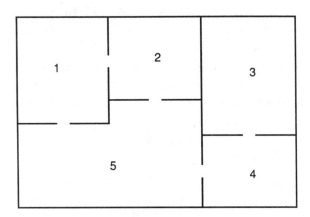

Figure 10: Maze for Problem 1

2. Suppose jar A contains 3 beads and jar B contains 4 beads. Of the 7 beads, 3 are red and 4 are black. We start a Markov process by picking at random one bead from each jar and interchanging them (that is, the bead from jar A is placed in jar B, and the bead from jar B is placed in jar A). This process is continued. Let the state of the process be identified by the number of red beads in jar A. State 0 represents 0 red beads in jar A, state 1 represents 1 red bead in jar A, state 2 represents 2 red beads in jar A, and state 3 represents 3 red beads in jar A.

   (a) Find the transition matrix for this process, focusing on the number of red beads in jar A.

   (b) If we start with the 3 red beads in A and the 4 black beads in B, what is the probability that there will be 2 red beads in jar A after 3 transitions?

(c) In the long run, what is the probability that there will be 2 red beads in jar A?

3. Wade, Donald, and Andrea are playing frisbee. Wade always throws to Donald, Donald always throws to Andrea, but Andrea is equally likely to throw to Wade or Donald.

   (a) Represent this information as a transition matrix of a Markov Chain.

   (b) Notice that this transition matrix has zero entries in several places. Compare the values of the transition matrix if raised to the second, fourth, sixth, and tenth powers. Are the zero entries still there? Can you explain?

4. The snack bar at school sells three items that students especially like: onion rings, french fries, and chocolate chip cookies. The manager noticed that what each student ordered depended on what he or she ordered on the last previous visit. She ran a survey during the first two weeks of school and found out that 50% of those who ordered onion rings on their last snack break ordered them again this time, while 35% switched to french fries, and 15% switched to chocolate chip cookies. Forty percent of those who ordered french fries on their last visit did so the next time, but 30% switched to onion rings, and another 30% switched to chocolate chip cookies. Of the students who ordered chocolate chip cookies on their last visit, 20% switched to onion rings, and 55% switched to french fries.

   (a) Set up the transition matrix for this Markov process.

   (b) On Monday, 30 students buy french fries, 40 buy onion rings, and 25 buy chocolate chip cookies. If these same students come in on Tuesday and each buys one of these items, how many orders of french fries should the manager expect to sell?

   (c) Suppose the students in part 4b continue buying from the snack bar every day for two weeks. How many orders of onion rings, french fries, and cookies should the manager expect to sell on the third Monday?

   (d) If these same people come all year, how many orders of onion rings, french fries, and cookies should the manager expect to sell to them each day?

   (e) In the long run, what percent of the orders for these three items will be onion rings? French fries? Chocolate chip cookies?

5. The manager of the snack bar in the previous problem decided to add soft custard ice-cream cones to the menu. Lots of students tried the new item, but few of them liked it. (The machine didn't work right and the ice cream came out lumpy.) A two-week survey gave the results in the transition matrix below.

	Rings	Fries	Cookies	Cones
Rings	0.4	0.3	0.1	0.2
Fries	0.25	0.35	0.2	0.2
Cookies	0.15	0.4	0.2	0.25
Cones	0.3	0.35	0.3	0.05

   (a) Does this system reach a stable state?

(b) If everyone really dislikes the ice cream, why does the stable state matrix show that many students still buy it?

(c) Why is a Markov chain not a good model for this system? Are people likely to forget that they did not like something only two days after they ate it? (Recall the principal assumption of a Markov process.) Why would this model work if the customers liked the ice cream?

6. A mouse is in the maze shown in Figure 11. Doors are shown by openings between rooms. Arrows indicate one-way doors and the direction of passage through the one-way doors. The mouse does not have to change rooms at each transition, but can stay in a room. Notice some of the rooms are impossible to leave once they are entered. During each transition, the mouse has an equal chance of leaving a room by a particular door or staying in the room. For example, during a single transition, a mouse in room 2 has a 1 in 6 chance of moving to room 1, a 1 in 6 chance of staying in room 2, a 1 in 3 chance of moving to room 3, and a 1 in 3 chance of moving to room 4.

(a) Find the transition matrix which describes the movement of the mouse.

(b) If the mouse starts in room 4, what is the probability that it will eventually be trapped in room 1?

(c) In which room besides 7 should the mouse be started to have the best chance of being trapped in room 7? Besides 1, the worst chance?

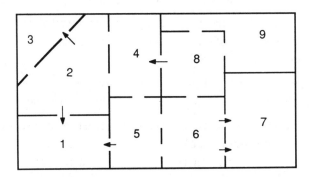

Figure 11: Maze for Problem 6

7. A research article [A. W. Marshall and H. Goldhamer, "An Application of Markov Processes to the Study of the Epidemiology of Mental Diseases," *American Statistical Association Journal*, March 1955, pp. 99-129] on the application of Markov chains to mental illness suggests that we consider a person to be in one of four states:

- state I—severely insane and hospitalized
- state II—dead, with death occurring while unhospitalized
- state III—sane

- state IV—insane and unhospitalized

For this model, assume that states I and II are absorbing states. Suppose that of the people in state III, after one year, 1.994% will be in state II, 98% will be in state III, and 0.006% will be in state IV. Also suppose that of the people in state IV, after one year, 2% will be in state I, 3% will be in state II, and 95% will be in state IV.

(a) Set up the transition matrix that describes this model.

(b) Find the stable state matrix.

(c) Determine the probability that a person who is currently well eventually will be severely insane and hospitalized.

8. Every census gives statisticians many new ideas to investigate. In the 1980 census a question was asked about the occupations of the fathers surveyed. Of the fathers who were professionals, 63% of their sons were professionals and 20% of their sons were in service-oriented jobs. Among fathers in service-oriented jobs, 31% of their sons were professionals and 45% worked in service jobs. Among fathers who worked in manufacturing, only 18% of their sons followed their profession and 41% went into service-oriented jobs.

(a) Based on the 1980 census, if John's great-grandfather was in a service-oriented job, what is the probability that John will also be in a service-oriented job?

(b) Suppose the 1980 census showed that 32% of the men were in manufacturing, 41% were professionals, and 27% were in service jobs. In ten generations, what percentage of the population of descendants will be professionals?

9. Go to the library and determine whether the presidents elected during the twentieth century, starting with Theodore Roosevelt, were Democrats or Republicans. Start with Theodore Roosevelt and note that Gerald Ford was not elected. The election process can be viewed as a Markov chain—each new election is a transition and the states of the process are Democrat and Republican. Design a transition matrix based on the probability of electing Democratic and Republican presidents in the twentieth century. In the transition matrix, count each president only once—a re-election is not considered a transition. According to your matrix, will a Republican or Democrat be elected in the next presidential election? When the year 2001 comes around, to what party will our president belong? What is the main weakness with this model of presidential elections?

10. A dreaded strain of flu is studied by research biologists. Statistics are taken each week in an effort to describe the probabilities after exposure of staying well, getting ill, becoming immune, and dying. A person becomes immune to this flu by having a mild case of it. Any well person once exposed to this flu has a 20% chance of getting the illness. Once a person becomes ill there is a 55% chance of remaining ill for more than a week, a 40% chance of being permanently immune after a mild illness, and a 5% chance of dying from the illness.

(a) Construct a transition matrix to represent the information above.

(b) Compute the probability of becoming immune after ten weeks for groups that begin as follows:

    i. 100% well and exposed

    ii. 50% well and 50% sick

    iii. 80% well and 20% immune

    iv. 100% sick

(c) Does this Markov process have a stable state?

11. Suppose that for the past several seasons you have been an avid fan of soccer. During the UNC versus Duke game you decide to follow the ball visually as it travels across the field. To make this easier you divide the field into 9 regions, according to the diagram in Figure 12. Your observations lead to the following data:

- When the ball is in area 1, 50% of the time it is kicked into area 3, 10% of the time into area 5, 20% into area 2, and 20% into area 4.

- From area 2, 50% of the time it moves into area 4, 15% of the time into area 6, and 35% into area 1.

- From area 3, it travels into areas 5, 7, 1, and 2 on 30%, 20%, 20%, and 30%, respectively, of the kicks.

- When in area 4, the ball is kicked 25% of the time into area 6, 25% of the time into area 2, 40% into area 1, and 10% into the goal (area 8).

- If the ball enters area 5, a goal is scored (area 9) 5% of the time; otherwise, it travels 35% of the time into area 7, 40% of the time into area 3, 10% into area 1, and 10% into area 2.

- From area 6, a goal is scored 20% of the time; the ball moves out to areas 4, 2, 1, and 3 on 25%, 10%, 25%, and 20%, respectively, of the kicks.

- If the ball enters area 7, a goal is scored 15% of the time, or the ball moves out to areas 5, 3, 1, and 2 on 50%, 20%, 10%, and 5%, respectively, of the ensuing kicks.

- The goals acted as absorbing states.

Given that the ball starts in area 1, find the probability that Duke will score.

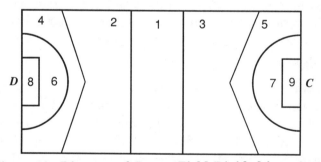

Figure 12: Diagram of Soccer Field Divided into Areas

12. An ant walks from one corner to another of a square *ABCD*. Assume that between successive observations of the process, the ant has moved one corner. The transition probabilities between corners are shown in Figure 13. Construct a Markov chain model for this situation.

(a) Investigate the behavior of successive powers of the transition matrix for this Markov chain. In successive powers, notice the oscillation of the transition probabilities between states represented by the rows of the powers of the transition matrix.

(b) What percentage of the time will the ant spend at each of the corners?

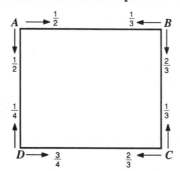

Figure 13: Ant Walking around a Square

7 Computer Graphics

The applications of computer graphics are commonplace. We see them everyday in newspapers, in magazines, on television, and in video games. This section focuses on the use of matrices and matrix operations in the implementation of computer graphics. It differs from previous sections in that it places greater emphasis on abstraction and results. For individuals who enjoy computer programming, this section can be the basis for many worthwhile projects and interesting investigations. A basic knowledge of trigonometry (right-triangle definitions of sine and cosine, addition formulas for sine and cosine) is a prerequisite for this section.

7.1 Rotations in Two Dimensions

Suppose we rotate a set of points in the plane through an angle θ. (An angle θ is considered positive if the direction of rotation is counterclockwise.) If a point P has coordinates (x, y), what are the coordinates (x', y') of the new point P' after rotation by a positive θ?

Referring to the graph in Figure 14, assume the point P is located in the first quadrant along ray $\overrightarrow{OP}$ at a distance r from the origin and at an angle α to the positive x-axis. We can express the coordinates of P in terms of r and α as follows:

$$x = r\cos\alpha$$
$$y = r\sin\alpha$$

(If you have studied polar coordinates, you will notice that these are the equations used to transform a point from polar coordinates (r, α) to rectangular coordinates (x, y).)

The point P' is also a distance r from the origin, but on $\overrightarrow{OP'}$ at an angle θ to $\overrightarrow{OP}$. Since $\overrightarrow{OP'}$ is at an angle $\theta + \alpha$ to the x-axis, the coordinates of P' can be expressed as follows:

$$x' = r\cos(\theta + \alpha)$$
$$y' = r\sin(\theta + \alpha)$$

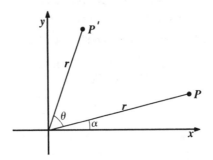

Figure 14: Rotation of a Point in the Plane

Using the trigonometric identities for the sine and cosine of the sum of two angles leads to

$$
\begin{aligned}
x' &= r\cos\theta\cos\alpha - r\sin\theta\sin\alpha \\
y' &= r\sin\theta\cos\alpha + r\cos\theta\sin\alpha,
\end{aligned}
$$

which can be rearranged as

$$
\begin{aligned}
x' &= (r\cos\alpha)\cos\theta - (r\sin\alpha)\sin\theta \\
y' &= (r\cos\alpha)\sin\theta + (r\sin\alpha)\cos\theta.
\end{aligned}
$$

Substitution for the original x- and y-values, $x = r\cos\alpha$ and $y = r\sin\alpha$, yields the following equations for transforming (x, y) to (x', y') through a rotation by θ:

$$
\begin{aligned}
x' &= x\cos\theta - y\sin\theta \\
y' &= x\sin\theta + y\cos\theta
\end{aligned}
$$

This set of equations for rotating a point in the plane can be conveniently represented with matrix multiplication as

$$
\begin{pmatrix} x' \\ y' \end{pmatrix} = \begin{pmatrix} \cos\theta & -\sin\theta \\ \sin\theta & \cos\theta \end{pmatrix} \begin{pmatrix} x \\ y \end{pmatrix}.
$$

The efficiency of matrix representation is apparent if we wish to rotate a set of n points in the plane, such as the vertices of a many-sided polygon. Instead of using n pairs of $(x, y) \rightarrow (x', y')$ transformation equations, the following single matrix equation will accomplish the rotation of all n points:

$$
\begin{pmatrix} x_1' & x_2' & \cdots & x_n' \\ y_1' & y_2' & \cdots & y_n' \end{pmatrix} = \begin{pmatrix} \cos\theta & -\sin\theta \\ \sin\theta & \cos\theta \end{pmatrix} \begin{pmatrix} x_1 & x_2 & \cdots & x_n \\ y_1 & y_2 & \cdots & y_n \end{pmatrix}
$$

If we let R represent the rotation matrix, specifically,

$$
R = \begin{pmatrix} \cos\theta & -\sin\theta \\ \sin\theta & \cos\theta \end{pmatrix},
$$

then notice that

$$R^2 = \begin{pmatrix} \cos^2\theta - \sin^2\theta & -2\sin\theta\cos\theta \\ 2\sin\theta\cos\theta & \cos^2\theta - \sin^2\theta \end{pmatrix}$$

$$= \begin{pmatrix} \cos 2\theta & -\sin 2\theta \\ \sin 2\theta & \cos 2\theta \end{pmatrix}.$$

Comparing the entries in R and R^2 reveals that R differs from R^2 only in that θ has been replaced by 2θ. Since the argument of the sine and cosine functions in R is the angle of rotation, R^2 must produce a rotation through an angle 2θ. This result indicates that successive rotations by θ can be implemented through successive multiplications by matrix R.

Also notice that if we let

$$R_1 = \begin{pmatrix} \cos\theta_1 & -\sin\theta_1 \\ \sin\theta_1 & \cos\theta_1 \end{pmatrix}$$

and

$$R_2 = \begin{pmatrix} \cos\theta_2 & -\sin\theta_2 \\ \sin\theta_2 & \cos\theta_2 \end{pmatrix},$$

then

$$R_1 R_2 = \begin{pmatrix} \cos\theta_1\cos\theta_2 - \sin\theta_1\sin\theta_2 & -\cos\theta_1\sin\theta_2 - \sin\theta_1\cos\theta_2 \\ \sin\theta_1\cos\theta_2 + \cos\theta_1\sin\theta_2 & \cos\theta_1\cos\theta_2 - \sin\theta_1\sin\theta_2 \end{pmatrix}$$

$$= \begin{pmatrix} \cos(\theta_1+\theta_2) & -\sin(\theta_1+\theta_2) \\ \sin(\theta_1+\theta_2) & \cos(\theta_1+\theta_2) \end{pmatrix}.$$

Comparing the result of $R_1 R_2$ with the general form of R shows that the angle θ in R has been replaced by $\theta_1 + \theta_2$; therefore, the final matrix above produces a rotation by an angle $\theta_1 + \theta_2$. The matrix R_1 represents a rotation through an angle θ_1; R_2 represents a rotation through an angle θ_2. The final form of $R_1 R_2$ indicates that successive rotations by θ_1 and θ_2, or a total rotation of $\theta_1 + \theta_2$, can be implemented through successive matrix multiplications by R_1 and R_2.

7.2 Homogeneous Coordinates

Rotation of coordinates can be accomplished through multiplication by the matrix R. A much simpler transformation of coordinates in the plane is represented by the following equations:

$$\begin{aligned} x' &= x + a \\ y' &= y + b \end{aligned}$$

This transformation, called a *translation* through (a, b), corresponds to shifting a point a units in the x-direction and b units in the y-direction. A translation can be implemented with matrices using the equation

$$\begin{pmatrix} x \\ y \end{pmatrix} + \begin{pmatrix} a \\ b \end{pmatrix} = \begin{pmatrix} x + a \\ y + b \end{pmatrix}.$$

The matrix equation for translating n points through (a, b) is

$$\begin{pmatrix} x_1 & x_2 & \cdots & x_n \\ y_1 & y_2 & \cdots & y_n \end{pmatrix} + \begin{pmatrix} a & a & \cdots & a \\ b & b & \cdots & b \end{pmatrix} = \begin{pmatrix} x_1 + a & x_2 + a & \cdots & x_n + a \\ y_1 + b & y_2 + b & \cdots & y_n + b \end{pmatrix}.$$

We have now implemented translations through matrix addition; however, we can also translate coordinates by using matrix multiplication. Multiplying the matrix

$$\begin{pmatrix} x \\ y \end{pmatrix}$$

by any matrix will not accomplish our task because the matrix equation

$$A \begin{pmatrix} x \\ y \end{pmatrix} = \begin{pmatrix} x + a \\ y + b \end{pmatrix}$$

has no solution for A. Mathematicians have found by "playing around" with this problem that expanding the dimensions of the matrices leads to a matrix multiplication version for translation of coordinates. The rationale for implementing translations with matrix multiplication will become clearer later in this section.

If the matrix representation of the coordinates (x, y) is changed to

$$\begin{pmatrix} x \\ y \\ 1 \end{pmatrix},$$

then translation of (x, y) by (a, b) corresponds to the multiplication

$$\begin{pmatrix} 1 & 0 & a \\ 0 & 1 & b \\ 0 & 0 & 1 \end{pmatrix} \begin{pmatrix} x \\ y \\ 1 \end{pmatrix} = \begin{pmatrix} x + a \\ y + b \\ 1 \end{pmatrix}.$$

Likewise, translation of n points corresponds to

$$\begin{pmatrix} 1 & 0 & a \\ 0 & 1 & b \\ 0 & 0 & 1 \end{pmatrix} \begin{pmatrix} x_1 & x_2 & \cdots & x_n \\ y_1 & y_2 & \cdots & y_n \\ 1 & 1 & \cdots & 1 \end{pmatrix} = \begin{pmatrix} x_1 + a & x_2 + a & \cdots & x_n + a \\ y_1 + b & y_2 + b & \cdots & y_n + b \\ 1 & 1 & \cdots & 1 \end{pmatrix}.$$

Adding a third row containing a 1 to the matrix representation for the point (x, y) provides a new coordinate system called *homogeneous coordinates*. In general, homogeneous coordinates are not required to contain a 1 in the bottom row of the matrix. If h is the number in the bottom row, then the point (x, y) corresponds to the homogeneous coordinates

$$\begin{pmatrix} hx \\ hy \\ h \end{pmatrix}.$$

For example, the homogeneous coordinates

$$\begin{pmatrix} 16 \\ 10 \\ 4 \end{pmatrix}$$

represent the point $(4, \frac{5}{2})$ in the plane.

Homogeneous coordinates for a specific point are not unique. For example, the point $(5, 3)$ can be represented in homogeneous coordinates by

$$\begin{pmatrix} 5 \\ 3 \\ 1 \end{pmatrix}$$

or, equivalently, by

$$\begin{pmatrix} 10 \\ 6 \\ 2 \end{pmatrix}.$$

On the other hand, the homogeneous coordinates

$$\begin{pmatrix} 7 \\ 4 \\ 2 \end{pmatrix}$$

represent the point $(\frac{7}{2}, 2)$, as do the homogeneous coordinates

$$\begin{pmatrix} 7/4 \\ 1 \\ 1/2 \end{pmatrix}.$$

In addition to allowing translations to be done with matrix multiplication, homogeneous coordinates can be used for scaling operations. *Scaling* refers to changing the size of an object according to a fixed proportion. If a set of n points corresponds to the vertices of a polygon, then the polygon is scaled by a factor of 2 by multiplying the x- and y-coordinates of the n points by 2, which doubles the size of the polygon. With matrices, this can be accomplished by either (a) multiplying the matrix of nonhomogeneous coordinates by a scalar 2 or (b) changing the bottom entry in the homogeneous coordinates to $1/2$. The second option is accomplished by the matrix multiplication shown below.

$$\begin{pmatrix} 1 & 0 & 0 \\ 0 & 1 & 0 \\ 0 & 0 & 1/2 \end{pmatrix} \begin{pmatrix} x_1 & x_2 & \cdots & x_n \\ y_1 & y_2 & \cdots & y_n \\ 1 & 1 & \cdots & 1 \end{pmatrix} = \begin{pmatrix} x_1 & x_2 & \cdots & x_n \\ y_1 & y_2 & \cdots & y_n \\ 1/2 & 1/2 & \cdots & 1/2 \end{pmatrix}$$

The homogeneous coordinates

$$\begin{pmatrix} x \\ y \\ 1/2 \end{pmatrix}$$

correspond to the point $(2x, 2y)$; therefore, the multiplication above corresponds to transforming all points (x_i, y_i) to $(2x_i, 2y_i)$. The distances between all pairs of points are doubled.

Example 1: To halve the size of a figure, left-multiply the matrix of homogeneous coordinates by

$$\begin{pmatrix} 1 & 0 & 0 \\ 0 & 1 & 0 \\ 0 & 0 & 2 \end{pmatrix}.$$

The effect of multiplication by this matrix on the points $(1, 2)$ and $(3, 7)$ is shown below.

$$\begin{pmatrix} 1 & 0 & 0 \\ 0 & 1 & 0 \\ 0 & 0 & 2 \end{pmatrix} \begin{pmatrix} 1 & 3 \\ 2 & 7 \\ 1 & 1 \end{pmatrix} = \begin{pmatrix} 1 & 3 \\ 2 & 7 \\ 2 & 2 \end{pmatrix}$$

The right side of the equation gives homogeneous coordinates for the points $(1/2, 1)$ and $(3/2, 7/2)$ in the plane, so the coordinates of the original points have been halved.

■

Now that we have examined translations and scaling in homogeneous coordinates, how are rotations accomplished with homogeneous coordinates? If the point (x, y), represented by

$$\begin{pmatrix} x \\ y \\ 1 \end{pmatrix},$$

is rotated by θ to the point (x', y'), represented by

$$\begin{pmatrix} x' \\ y' \\ 1 \end{pmatrix},$$

then the transformation equations relating (x, y) and (x', y') are the same as in section 7.1. Inserting the 2×2 rotation matrix from section 7.1 in a 3×3 matrix and multiplying by the homogeneous coordinates for (x, y) yields

$$\begin{pmatrix} \cos\theta & -\sin\theta & 0 \\ \sin\theta & \cos\theta & 0 \\ 0 & 0 & 1 \end{pmatrix} \begin{pmatrix} x \\ y \\ 1 \end{pmatrix} = \begin{pmatrix} x\cos\theta - y\sin\theta \\ x\sin\theta + y\cos\theta \\ 1 \end{pmatrix}$$

$$= \begin{pmatrix} x' \\ y' \\ 1 \end{pmatrix},$$

where (x', y') corresponds to the rotation of (x, y) through an angle θ.

With homogeneous coordinates, matrix multiplication can be used to implement the translation, scaling, and rotation of points in the plane. In section 7.1, we observed that successive rotations correspond to successive matrix multiplications. Similarly, translation, scaling, and rotation can be performed in sequence through successive multiplication by the appropriate matrices.

Example 2: Transform the point in the plane $(2,5)$ by scaling by a factor 2, then translating through $(-1,3)$.

The matrices that accomplish these transformations are shown below. Notice that the matrix for the second transformation, the translation, is placed to the left of the matrix for the first transformation, the scaling.

$$\begin{pmatrix} 1 & 0 & -1 \\ 0 & 1 & 3 \\ 0 & 0 & 1 \end{pmatrix} \begin{pmatrix} 1 & 0 & 0 \\ 0 & 1 & 0 \\ 0 & 0 & 1/2 \end{pmatrix} \begin{pmatrix} 2 \\ 5 \\ 1 \end{pmatrix}$$

Multiplying the two transformation matrices yields

$$\begin{pmatrix} 1 & 0 & -1/2 \\ 0 & 1 & 3/2 \\ 0 & 0 & 1/2 \end{pmatrix} \begin{pmatrix} 2 \\ 5 \\ 1 \end{pmatrix}.$$

Completing the multiplication results in the matrix

$$\begin{pmatrix} 3/2 \\ 13/2 \\ 1/2 \end{pmatrix},$$

which corresponds to the point in the plane with coordinates $(3,13)$. Is this the result we should expect? Scaling $(2,5)$ by a factor of 2 transforms the point to $(4,10)$. A subsequent translation through $(-1,3)$ gives us the point $(3,13)$—the result obtained by matrix multiplication.

Reversing the order of the transformations—translating first and then scaling—leads to the calculations shown below.

$$\begin{pmatrix} 1 & 0 & 0 \\ 0 & 1 & 0 \\ 0 & 0 & 1/2 \end{pmatrix} \begin{pmatrix} 1 & 0 & -1 \\ 0 & 1 & 3 \\ 0 & 0 & 1 \end{pmatrix} \begin{pmatrix} 2 \\ 5 \\ 1 \end{pmatrix} = \begin{pmatrix} 1 & 0 & -1 \\ 0 & 1 & 3 \\ 0 & 0 & 1/2 \end{pmatrix} \begin{pmatrix} 2 \\ 5 \\ 1 \end{pmatrix}$$

$$= \begin{pmatrix} 1 \\ 8 \\ 1/2 \end{pmatrix}$$

The transformed homogeneous coordinates represent the point in the plane with coordinates $(2,16)$, which corresponds to translating $(2,5)$ through $(-1,3)$ (yielding the point $(1,8)$) and then scaling by 2 (resulting in the point $(2,16)$). Changing the order of the transformations leads to different results. Evidently, reversing the order of the transformations causes the translation to be scaled by 2. (Observe that scaling the original coordinates $(2,5)$ by 2 and then translating through $(-2,6)$ yields the point $(2,16)$.) Indeed, one expects that changing the order of the transformation matrices would change the final results, since matrix multiplication is not commutative.

The concepts illustrated in Example 2 can be expanded by examining the following more general situation: Transform a point (x, y) by first scaling by a factor k, then translating through (a, b).

To accomplish these transformations, we use the matrix multiplication shown below.

$$\begin{pmatrix} 1 & 0 & a \\ 0 & 1 & b \\ 0 & 0 & 1 \end{pmatrix} \begin{pmatrix} 1 & 0 & 0 \\ 0 & 1 & 0 \\ 0 & 0 & 1/k \end{pmatrix} \begin{pmatrix} x \\ y \\ 1 \end{pmatrix}$$

This multiplication simplifies to

$$\begin{pmatrix} 1 & 0 & a/k \\ 0 & 1 & b/k \\ 0 & 0 & 1/k \end{pmatrix} \begin{pmatrix} x \\ y \\ 1 \end{pmatrix},$$

which results in

$$\begin{pmatrix} x + a/k \\ y + b/k \\ 1/k \end{pmatrix}.$$

The final matrix corresponds to the point in the plane with coordinates $(kx + a, ky + b)$. This is the result we expected—a scaling by k and a translation through (a, b).

Example 3: Combine the following transformations: scale by a factor k, rotate by an angle θ, then translate through (a, b). The matrix multiplication that accomplishes the transformations in the order stated are shown below.

$$\begin{pmatrix} 1 & 0 & a \\ 0 & 1 & b \\ 0 & 0 & 1 \end{pmatrix} \begin{pmatrix} \cos\theta & -\sin\theta & 0 \\ \sin\theta & \cos\theta & 0 \\ 0 & 0 & 1 \end{pmatrix} \begin{pmatrix} 1 & 0 & 0 \\ 0 & 1 & 0 \\ 0 & 0 & 1/k \end{pmatrix} \begin{pmatrix} x \\ y \\ 1 \end{pmatrix}$$

$$= \begin{pmatrix} 1 & 0 & a \\ 0 & 1 & b \\ 0 & 0 & 1 \end{pmatrix} \begin{pmatrix} \cos\theta & -\sin\theta & 0 \\ \sin\theta & \cos\theta & 0 \\ 0 & 0 & 1/k \end{pmatrix} \begin{pmatrix} x \\ y \\ 1 \end{pmatrix}$$

$$= \begin{pmatrix} \cos\theta & -\sin\theta & a/k \\ \sin\theta & \cos\theta & b/k \\ 0 & 0 & 1/k \end{pmatrix} \begin{pmatrix} x \\ y \\ 1 \end{pmatrix}$$

$$= \begin{pmatrix} x\cos\theta - y\sin\theta + a/k \\ x\sin\theta + y\sin\theta + b/k \\ 1/k \end{pmatrix}$$

$$= \begin{pmatrix} x' + a/k \\ y' + b/k \\ 1/k \end{pmatrix}$$

The point (x', y') corresponds to the rotation of (x, y) through an angle θ. The final transformed homogeneous coordinates correspond to the point in the plane $(kx' + a, ky' + b)$. The result is the point (x, y) rotated through an angle θ, scaled by a factor k, and translated through (a, b).

The results above demonstrate that the single matrix

$$\begin{pmatrix} \cos\theta & -\sin\theta & a/k \\ \sin\theta & \cos\theta & b/k \\ 0 & 0 & 1/k \end{pmatrix}$$

performs a scaling by k, a rotation by θ, and a translation through (a,b) when it left-multiplies a matrix of points given in homogeneous coordinates.

Our intuition suggests that rotation and scaling are independent and can be performed in either order. This observation can be demonstrated mathematically by noting that the transformation matrices for rotation and for scaling are commutative with respect to multiplication, as shown below.

$$\begin{pmatrix} \cos\theta & -\sin\theta & 0 \\ \sin\theta & \cos\theta & 0 \\ 0 & 0 & 1 \end{pmatrix} \begin{pmatrix} 1 & 0 & 0 \\ 0 & 1 & 0 \\ 0 & 0 & 1/k \end{pmatrix} = \begin{pmatrix} \cos\theta & -\sin\theta & 0 \\ \sin\theta & \cos\theta & 0 \\ 0 & 0 & 1/k \end{pmatrix}$$

$$\begin{pmatrix} 1 & 0 & 0 \\ 0 & 1 & 0 \\ 0 & 0 & 1/k \end{pmatrix} \begin{pmatrix} \cos\theta & -\sin\theta & 0 \\ \sin\theta & \cos\theta & 0 \\ 0 & 0 & 1 \end{pmatrix} = \begin{pmatrix} \cos\theta & -\sin\theta & 0 \\ \sin\theta & \cos\theta & 0 \\ 0 & 0 & 1/k \end{pmatrix}$$

∎

Homogeneous coordinates provide a unified, compact notation for transformations. Translation, scaling, and rotation can all be represented with matrix multiplication; the matrix associated with the last transformation is positioned farthest to the left. In Examples 2 and 3, we have seen that finding the product of a set of transformation matrices leads to a single matrix with parameters corresponding to the desired transformations. Once a matrix is derived that implements a series of transformations, the parameters can be replaced by actual values, and a single matrix multiplication can be used to transform a set of points.

7.3   Exercises

Determine the sequence of matrices that can be multiplied to perform the following transformations in the plane. Use these matrices to find the new coordinates under each transformation of the vertices $A(2,1)$, $B(1.5,2)$, and $C(3,4)$ of $\triangle ABC$.

1. Reflect over the x-axis.

2. Reflect over the y-axis.

3. Triple in size, rotate $75°$, and translate by $(-3,-2)$.

4. Translate through $(-2,-1)$, rotate $-45°$, and then scale by a factor of $1/2$.

7.4   Transformations in Three Dimensions

The concepts of homogeneous coordinates and transformations in two dimensions can be extended quite naturally to three dimensions. A set of homogeneous coordinates for a point (x, y, z) in 3-space are

$$\begin{pmatrix} x \\ y \\ z \\ 1 \end{pmatrix}.$$

All homogeneous coordinates for (x, y, z) are of the form

$$\begin{pmatrix} hx \\ hy \\ hz \\ h \end{pmatrix}.$$

Generalizing the results of the previous section, scaling by a factor k is accomplished by left-multiplying by the matrix

$$\begin{pmatrix} 1 & 0 & 0 & 0 \\ 0 & 1 & 0 & 0 \\ 0 & 0 & 1 & 0 \\ 0 & 0 & 0 & 1/k \end{pmatrix}.$$

Translation through (a, b, c) is performed by left-multiplying by the matrix

$$\begin{pmatrix} 1 & 0 & 0 & a \\ 0 & 1 & 0 & b \\ 0 & 0 & 1 & c \\ 0 & 0 & 0 & 1 \end{pmatrix}.$$

Rotations in three dimensions are similar to the two-dimensional case in that the rotation occurs in a plane. We will consider the three cases of rotations in the coordinate planes, as shown in Figure 15.

1. Rotation in the xy-plane, about the z-axis: If we assume that positive θ is in the direction from the x-axis to the y-axis, then the transformations of x and y are the same as in the two-dimensional case. The value of z should not change. We wish to make the following transformation:

$$\begin{aligned} x' &= x \cos\theta - y \sin\theta \\ y' &= x \sin\theta + y \cos\theta \\ z' &= z \end{aligned}$$

The matrix that implements these equations using homogeneous coordinates is shown below.

$$\begin{pmatrix} \cos\theta & -\sin\theta & 0 & 0 \\ \sin\theta & \cos\theta & 0 & 0 \\ 0 & 0 & 1 & 0 \\ 0 & 0 & 0 & 1 \end{pmatrix} \begin{pmatrix} x \\ y \\ z \\ 1 \end{pmatrix} = \begin{pmatrix} x \cos\theta - y \sin\theta \\ x \sin\theta + y \cos\theta \\ z \\ 1 \end{pmatrix}$$

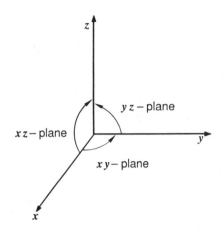

Figure 15: Rotations in the Coordinate Planes in Three Dimensions

$$= \begin{pmatrix} x' \\ y' \\ z' \\ 1 \end{pmatrix}$$

2. Rotation in the xz-plane, about the y-axis: Assume that positive θ is in the direction from the x-axis to the z-axis. The value of y must remain constant. The problem involves a rearrangement of the variables from the first case, with y changed to z and z changed to y; therefore, we wish to make the following transformation:

$$\begin{aligned} x' &= x\cos\theta - z\sin\theta \\ y' &= y \\ z' &= x\sin\theta + z\cos\theta \end{aligned}$$

The rotation is accomplished by the matrix multiplication shown below.

$$\begin{pmatrix} \cos\theta & 0 & -\sin\theta & 0 \\ 0 & 1 & 0 & 0 \\ \sin\theta & 0 & \cos\theta & 0 \\ 0 & 0 & 0 & 1 \end{pmatrix} \begin{pmatrix} x \\ y \\ z \\ 1 \end{pmatrix} = \begin{pmatrix} x\cos\theta - z\sin\theta \\ y \\ x\sin\theta + z\cos\theta \\ 1 \end{pmatrix}$$

$$= \begin{pmatrix} x' \\ y' \\ z' \\ 1 \end{pmatrix}$$

3. Rotation in the yz-plane, about the x-axis: Assume that positive θ is in the direction from the y-axis to the z-axis. The value of x remains constant. Again we can rearrange the variables from case 1, changing x to y, changing y to z, and changing z to x. The following equations represent the required transformation:

$$\begin{aligned} x' &= x \\ y' &= y\cos\theta - z\sin\theta \\ z' &= y\sin\theta + z\cos\theta \end{aligned}$$

The matrix multiplication shown below accomplishes this rotation.

$$\begin{pmatrix} 1 & 0 & 0 & 0 \\ 0 & \cos\theta & -\sin\theta & 0 \\ 0 & \sin\theta & \cos\theta & 0 \\ 0 & 0 & 0 & 1 \end{pmatrix} \begin{pmatrix} x \\ y \\ z \\ 1 \end{pmatrix} = \begin{pmatrix} x \\ y\cos\theta - z\sin\theta \\ y\sin\theta + z\cos\theta \\ 1 \end{pmatrix}$$

$$= \begin{pmatrix} x' \\ y' \\ z' \\ 1 \end{pmatrix}$$

A final transformation will be discussed to complete this section. A computer screen is two-dimensional, so we must determine how to form the projection of a three-dimensional figure onto a plane. Although this seems complicated, for now we need only consider a single case: assume the observer is on the positive x-axis, and the projection is onto the yz-plane. Other situations can be handled by first performing rotations that move the observer onto the x-axis.

Let the situation be as shown in Figure 16. The projection of a point P onto the yz-plane is P' from the perspective of a viewer at V, which is k units from the origin on the x-axis. The 3-space coordinates for P are (x, y, z); for P' they are $(0, y', z')$. The foot of the perpendicular from P to the xy-plane is at Q. The foot of the perpendicular from P' to the xy-plane is at Q' on the y-axis. Assuming we know the values of x, y, z, and k, our task is to determine the values of y' and z'.

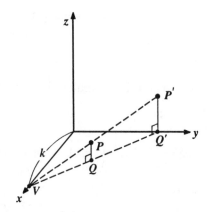

Figure 16: Projection of a Point onto the yz-Plane

The situation pictured in Figure 16 can be enhanced by introducing similar triangles as in Figure 17. The lengths of various sides of triangles are also shown. Equating ratios of corresponding sides, we see from $\triangle VOQ'$ that

$$\frac{VQ}{VQ'} = \frac{y}{y'} = \frac{k-x}{k}.$$

In $\triangle VQ'P'$, we observe that

$$\frac{VQ}{VQ'} = \frac{z}{z'}.$$

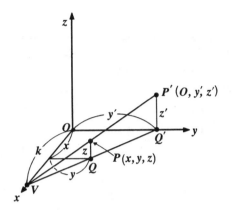

Figure 17: Projection with Relevant Similar Triangles

The previous two sets of ratios are equal; therefore,

$$\frac{y}{y'} = \frac{k - x}{k} = \frac{z}{z'}.$$

Solving for y' leads to

$$y' = \frac{ky}{k - x},$$

or

$$y' = \frac{y}{1 - \frac{x}{k}}.$$

Solving for z' yields

$$z' = \frac{kz}{k - x},$$

or

$$z' = \frac{z}{1 - \frac{x}{k}}.$$

The second form of the equations for y' and z' suggests that the new values are just the original values y and z scaled by a factor $1/(1 - \frac{x}{k})$. The matrix multiplication below scales y and z as required, as well as setting x' equal to 0.

$$\begin{pmatrix} 0 & 0 & 0 & 0 \\ 0 & 1 & 0 & 0 \\ 0 & 0 & 1 & 0 \\ -1/k & 0 & 0 & 1 \end{pmatrix} \begin{pmatrix} x \\ y \\ z \\ 1 \end{pmatrix} = \begin{pmatrix} 0 \\ y \\ z \\ 1 - \frac{x}{k} \end{pmatrix}$$

The resulting homogeneous coordinates correspond to the point located by the coordinates

$$\left(0, \frac{y}{1 - \frac{x}{k}}, \frac{z}{1 - \frac{x}{k}} \right)$$

in 3-space, which are the coordinates of $P'(0, y', z')$ that we set out to find.

Example: A cube is oriented in 3-space with corners at the points with coordinates $(0,0,0)$, $(5,0,0)$, $(0,5,0)$, $(0,0,5)$, $(5,5,0)$, $(5,0,5)$, $(0,5,5)$, and $(5,5,5)$. Determine the appearance of the cube from the point of view of an observer at $(10,10,15)$.

The cube and the location of the observer in 3-space are shown in Figure 18. The corners of the cube have been labeled with the letters A through H. To determine how the cube appears to the observer, we will find the projections of the corners of the cube onto the yz-plane and then draw the edges between adjacent corners.

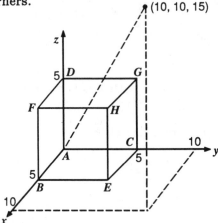

Figure 18: Orientation of the Cube and the Observer

To project the corners of the cube onto the yz-plane, we must first rotate the observer and the cube so that the observer is on the x-axis. The necessary angles of rotation are pictured in Figure 19. The first rotation θ_1 is $-45°$ in a plane parallel to the xy-plane. (Recall that a rotation in the xy-plane is negative if it proceeds from the y-axis to the x-axis.) This places the observer in the xz-plane as shown in Figure 19. The second rotation θ_2 is $-\tan^{-1}(15/10\sqrt{2})$ in the xz-plane. (Recall that a rotation in the xz-plane is negative if it proceeds from the z-axis to the x-axis.) This places the observer on the x-axis at a distance $\sqrt{425}$ from the origin as shown in Figure 19. After these rotations are accomplished, the cube can be projected onto the yz-plane using the projection matrix with $k = \sqrt{425}$.

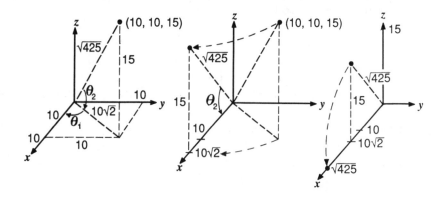

Figure 19: Rotation of the Observer from $(10,10,15)$ to the x-Axis

The matrix multiplication that performs the rotations by θ_1 and θ_2 and the projection onto the yz-plane is shown below.

$$
\begin{pmatrix}
0 & 0 & 0 & 0 \\
0 & 1 & 0 & 0 \\
0 & 0 & 1 & 0 \\
-1/k & 0 & 0 & 1
\end{pmatrix}
\begin{pmatrix}
\cos\theta_2 & 0 & -\sin\theta_2 & 0 \\
0 & 1 & 0 & 0 \\
\sin\theta_2 & 0 & \cos\theta_2 & 0 \\
0 & 0 & 0 & 1
\end{pmatrix}
\begin{pmatrix}
\cos\theta_1 & -\sin\theta_1 & 0 & 0 \\
\sin\theta_1 & \cos\theta_1 & 0 & 0 \\
0 & 0 & 1 & 0 \\
0 & 0 & 0 & 1
\end{pmatrix}
$$

The matrix of homogeneous coordinates for the corners of the cube is

$$
\begin{pmatrix}
0 & 5 & 0 & 0 & 5 & 5 & 0 & 5 \\
0 & 0 & 5 & 0 & 5 & 0 & 5 & 5 \\
0 & 0 & 0 & 5 & 0 & 5 & 5 & 5 \\
1 & 1 & 1 & 1 & 1 & 1 & 1 & 1
\end{pmatrix}.
$$

The transformation of the cube is accomplished by left-multiplying the matrix of homogeneous coordinates by the rotation and projection matrices shown above, using the appropriate values of θ_1, θ_2, and k. Performing this multiplication yields the product

$$
\begin{pmatrix}
0 & 0 & 0 & 0 & 0 & 0 & 0 & 0 \\
0 & -3.54 & 3.54 & 0 & 0 & -3.54 & 3.54 & 0 \\
0 & -2.57 & -2.57 & 3.43 & -5.14 & 0.86 & 0.86 & -1.71 \\
1 & 0.88 & 0.88 & 0.82 & 0.76 & 0.71 & 0.71 & 0.59
\end{pmatrix},
$$

which is the matrix of transformed homogeneous coordinates. These homogeneous coordinates correspond to the points in 3-space located by the coordinates:

$$(0,0,0), \quad (0,-4.02,-2.92), \quad (0,4.02,-2.92), \quad (0,0,4.18), \quad (0,0,-6.76),$$

$$(0,-4.99,1.21), \quad (0,4.99,1.21), \quad \text{and} \quad (0,0,-2.90)$$

A plot of these points in the yz-plane and the edges of the cube are shown in Figure 20, which thus illustrates the appearance of the cube to an observer at $(10,10,15)$.

∎

Many computer programming languages provide good support for matrix operations, and matrix multiplication can be implemented easily in such languages. In actual applications of computer graphics, speed and the ability to handle an object requiring a large number of points is critical. Some computers have been designed with this application in mind. Essentially, these computers are designed to perform many matrix computations simultaneously, instead of using a single arithmetic processor sequentially. Performing matrix computations simultaneously greatly increases the speed with which calculations are performed and enables the programmer to use higher resolution in graphics.

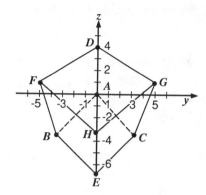

Figure 20: Appearance of the Cube to an Observer at $(10, 10, 15)$

7.5   Exercises

In Exercises 1–5, determine the sequence of matrices that can be multiplied to perform the following transformations in 3-space:

1. Reflect over the xz-plane.

2. Project onto the yz-plane from the point of view of an observer located at $(10, 0, 0)$.

3. Rotate 20° in the xy-plane, then rotate 45° in the yz-plane.

4. Double in size, translate through $(1, 2, -1)$, and project onto the yz-plane from the point of view of an observer at $(5, 0, 0)$.

5. Project onto the yz-plane from the point of view of an observer at $(10, 10, 10)$.

6. Use the transformation of Exercise 2 on the cube with corners at the points $(0, 0, 0)$, $(5, 0, 0)$, $(0, 5, 0)$, $(0, 0, 5)$, $(5, 5, 0)$, $(5, 0, 5)$, $(0, 5, 5)$, and $(5, 5, 5)$. Plot the coordinates of the transformed points in the yz-plane and draw the cube as it appears to the observer.

7. Draw a picture of the original cube of Exercise 6 as it appears to an observer at the point $(10, 4, 6)$. Do this by finding the projections of the corners onto the yz-plane and then drawing the edges of the cube.

8. Draw a picture of the original cube of Exercise 6 as it appears to an observer at the point $(10, 7, 8)$. Do this by finding the projections of the corners onto the yz-plane and then drawing the edges of the cube.

Answers to Exercises

Section 2.1 Exercises

1. (a) Campus Bookstore inventory:

$$
\begin{array}{c}
 \quad\; T \quad\;\; F \quad\;\; N \quad\;\; R \\
\begin{array}{c} H \\ P \end{array}
\left(
\begin{array}{cccc}
5280 & 1680 & 2320 & 1890 \\
1940 & 2810 & 1490 & 2070
\end{array}
\right)
\end{array}
$$

(b) College Bookstore inventory:

$$
\begin{array}{c}
 \quad\; T \quad\;\; F \quad\;\; N \quad\;\; R \\
\begin{array}{c} H \\ P \end{array}
\left(
\begin{array}{cccc}
6340 & 2220 & 1790 & 1980 \\
2050 & 3100 & 1720 & 2710
\end{array}
\right)
\end{array}
$$

(c) Total inventory:

$$
\begin{array}{c}
 \quad\;\; T \quad\;\;\; F \quad\;\;\; N \quad\;\;\; R \\
\begin{array}{c} H \\ P \end{array}
\left(
\begin{array}{cccc}
11620 & 3900 & 4110 & 3870 \\
3990 & 5910 & 3210 & 4780
\end{array}
\right)
\end{array}
$$

2. (a) End-of-first-quarter matrix:

$$
T = A + B - C =
\begin{array}{c}
 \quad\;\; c \quad\;\;\;\; s \quad\;\; m \\
\begin{array}{c} N \\ D \\ S \end{array}
\left(
\begin{array}{ccc}
42468 & 11541 & 528 \\
15890 & 8967 & 97 \\
26843 & 12723 & 104
\end{array}
\right)
\end{array}
$$

(b) End-of-second-quarter matrix:

$$
0.93T =
\begin{array}{c}
 \quad\;\; c \quad\;\;\;\; s \quad\;\; m \\
\begin{array}{c} N \\ D \\ S \end{array}
\left(
\begin{array}{ccc}
39496 & 10734 & 491 \\
14778 & 8340 & 91 \\
24964 & 11833 & 97
\end{array}
\right)
\end{array}
$$

(c) Merger of two banks:

$$
\begin{array}{c}
 \quad\;\; c \quad\;\;\;\; s \quad\;\; m \\
\begin{array}{c} N \\ D \\ S \end{array}
\left(
\begin{array}{ccc}
41384 & 12666 & 564 \\
16014 & 10738 & 242 \\
27718 & 14852 & 910
\end{array}
\right)
\end{array}
$$

Section 3.1 Exercises

1. MO: 2×1, MP: 2×2, PM: 2×2, MR: 2×2, RM: 2×2, NQ: 3×1, NU: 3×4, PO: 2×1, PR: 2×2, RP: 2×2, RO: 2×1, SM: 4×2, SO: 4×2, SP: 4×2, SR: 4×2, US: 3×2, UT: 3×1

2.

$$MP = PM = \begin{pmatrix} 1 & 0 \\ 0 & 1 \end{pmatrix}$$

3. Yes, matrix multiplication is associative. For example, $M(RP) = (MR)P$, as shown below. We find that

$$\begin{aligned} RP &= \begin{pmatrix} 3 & 1 \\ -1 & 0 \end{pmatrix} \begin{pmatrix} 0 & 1/2 \\ -1 & 1/2 \end{pmatrix} \\ &= \begin{pmatrix} -1 & 2 \\ 0 & -1/2 \end{pmatrix}, \end{aligned}$$

so that

$$\begin{aligned} M(RP) &= \begin{pmatrix} 1 & -1 \\ 2 & 0 \end{pmatrix} \begin{pmatrix} -1 & 2 \\ 0 & -1/2 \end{pmatrix} \\ &= \begin{pmatrix} -1 & 5/2 \\ -2 & 4 \end{pmatrix}. \end{aligned}$$

We also know that

$$\begin{aligned} MR &= \begin{pmatrix} 1 & -1 \\ 2 & 0 \end{pmatrix} \begin{pmatrix} 3 & 1 \\ -1 & 0 \end{pmatrix} \\ &= \begin{pmatrix} 4 & 1 \\ 6 & 2 \end{pmatrix}, \end{aligned}$$

so that

$$\begin{aligned} (MR)P &= \begin{pmatrix} 4 & 1 \\ 6 & 2 \end{pmatrix} \begin{pmatrix} 0 & 1/2 \\ -1 & 1/2 \end{pmatrix} \\ &= \begin{pmatrix} -1 & 5/2 \\ -2 & 4 \end{pmatrix}. \end{aligned}$$

Examining the results reveals that $M(RP) = (MR)P$.

4. Total earnings for each state (in millions of dollars):

$$\begin{pmatrix} Bonds & Mort. & Loans \\ 1.075 & 1.1125 & 1.06 \end{pmatrix} \begin{matrix} & NC & ND & NM \\ \begin{matrix} Bonds \\ Mort. \\ Loans \end{matrix} & \begin{pmatrix} 13 & 25 & 22 \\ 6 & 9 & 4 \\ 29 & 17 & 13 \end{pmatrix} \end{matrix} = \begin{matrix} NC & ND & NM \\ \begin{pmatrix} 3.39 & 3.9075 & 2.88 \end{pmatrix} \end{matrix}$$

5. Total value of the stocks (in dollars) at the end of each year:

$$
\begin{matrix}
& A & B & C \\
& (100 & 200 & 150)
\end{matrix}
\quad
\begin{matrix}
& & 1984 & 1985 & 1986 \\
A & \Big(& 68 & 72 & 75 \\
B & \Big| & 55 & 60 & 67.5 \\
C & \Big(& 82.5 & 84 & 87
\end{matrix}
\Big)
=
\begin{matrix}
1984 & 1985 & 1986 \\
(30,175 & 31,800 & 34,050)
\end{matrix}
$$

6. Sick males $= 79$, well females $= 38$, and female carriers $= 76$. These numbers are derived from the following matrix multiplication:

$$
\begin{matrix}
& Jr. & Sr. \\
Well & \Big(0.15 & 0.25 \Big) \\
Sick & \Big| 0.35 & 0.40 \Big| \\
Car. & \Big(0.50 & 0.35 \Big)
\end{matrix}
\quad
\begin{matrix}
& m & f \\
Jr. & \Big(104 & 80 \Big) \\
Sr. & \Big(107 & 103 \Big)
\end{matrix}
=
\begin{matrix}
& m & f \\
Well & \Big(42.35 & 37.75 \Big) \\
Sick & \Big| 79.2 & 69.2 \Big| \\
Car. & \Big(89.45 & 76.05 \Big)
\end{matrix}
$$

7. Define the matrices for the inventory parts (I) and the daily manufacturing goal (N) as

$$
I =
\begin{matrix}
& t & ca & co & d \\
B & \Big(50 & 30 & 7 & 3 \Big) \\
Ec & \Big| 65 & 50 & 9 & 4 \Big| \\
Ex & \Big| 85 & 42 & 10 & 6 \Big| \\
P & \Big(85 & 42 & 10 & 12 \Big)
\end{matrix}
\quad \text{and} \quad
N =
\begin{matrix}
B & Ec & Ex & P \\
(10 & 12 & 11 & 7)
\end{matrix}.
$$

(a) The answers are the results of the matrix multiplication

$$
NI =
\begin{matrix}
t & ca & co & d \\
(2810 & 1656 & 358 & 228)
\end{matrix}.
$$

(b) The new daily manufacturing goals are given by

$$
1.4N =
\begin{matrix}
B & Ec & Ex & P \\
(14 & 16.8 & 15.4 & 9.8)
\end{matrix},
$$

which should be rounded to integer quantities.

(c) Define a matrix H for hours of labor as

$$
H =
\begin{matrix}
& Hrs. \\
B & \Big(5 \Big) \\
Ec & \Big| 7 \Big| \\
Ex & \Big| 6 \Big| \\
P & \Big(7 \Big)
\end{matrix}.
$$

The number of labor hours needed per week is given by

$$
NH = 249.
$$

With 7-hour workdays, the number of employees needed is $249/7 = 35.6$, which implies that 36 employees are needed to maintain full production. For August and September, we want $(1.4NH)/7 = 348.6/7$, which rounds to 50.

8. For $\theta = 30°$, the new ordered pairs are found by the multiplication

$$\begin{pmatrix} \sqrt{3}/2 & -1/2 \\ 1/2 & \sqrt{3}/2 \end{pmatrix} \begin{pmatrix} x \\ y \end{pmatrix}.$$

The point $(1,0)$ is transformed to $(\sqrt{3}/2, 1/2)$; $(2,4)$ is changed to $(\sqrt{3}-2, 2\sqrt{3}+1)$; and $(3,0)$ becomes $(3\sqrt{3}/2, 3/2)$. Referring to the graph shown below, the original parabola appears to rotate $30°$ in the counterclockwise direction. We conjecture that the matrix produces a counterclockwise rotation through an angle θ. Using $\theta = 90°$ gives the rotation matrix

$$\begin{pmatrix} 0 & -1 \\ 1 & 0 \end{pmatrix},$$

which leads to the transformations

$$(1,0) \Rightarrow (0,1), \quad (2,4) \Rightarrow (-4,2), \quad \text{and} \quad (3,0) \Rightarrow (0,3).$$

The transformed coordinates reflect a rotation by $90°$, as shown in the coordinate system below.

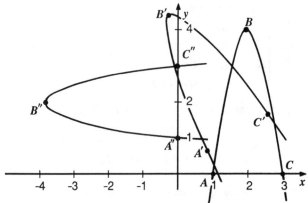

9. The goal for each branch in each type of account is given by the following matrix multiplication:

$$
\begin{array}{c}
\\ N \\ D \\ S
\end{array}
\begin{pmatrix}
c & s & m \\
40039 & 10135 & 512 \\
15231 & 8751 & 105 \\
25612 & 12187 & 97
\end{pmatrix}
\begin{array}{c}
\\ c \\ s \\ m
\end{array}
\begin{pmatrix}
c & s & m \\
1.21 & 0 & 0 \\
0 & 1.35 & 0 \\
0 & 0 & 1.52
\end{pmatrix}
=
\begin{array}{c}
\\ N \\ D \\ S
\end{array}
\begin{pmatrix}
c & s & m \\
48448 & 13683 & 779 \\
18430 & 11814 & 160 \\
30991 & 16453 & 148
\end{pmatrix}
$$

Right-multiplying this result by the matrix

$$\begin{pmatrix} 1 \\ 1 \\ 1 \end{pmatrix}$$

yields the following total number of accounts at each branch:

$$
\begin{array}{c}
 \\ N \\ D \\ S
\end{array}
\begin{pmatrix}
Total \\
62910 \\
30404 \\
47592
\end{pmatrix}
$$

10. (a) The maximum total score possible occurs when each of the five items receives a score of 10, for a total of $10(3 + 5 + 6 + 8 + 4) = 260$.

(b) Use matrix multiplication with a weight vector and a score vector:

$$
\begin{array}{c}
 \\
 \\
Wt.
\end{array}
\begin{array}{ccccc}
BR & EP & RP & PD & CI \\
\left(3 \right. & 5 & 6 & 8 & \left. 4 \right)
\end{array}
\quad
\begin{array}{c}
 \\
BR \\
EP \\
RP \\
PD \\
CI
\end{array}
\begin{array}{c}
Score \\
\left(\begin{array}{c} 8 \\ 9 \\ 7 \\ 8 \\ 6 \end{array} \right)
\end{array}
= \left(199 \right)
$$

(c) Extend part (b) with the following operation:

$$
\begin{array}{c}
 \\
 \\
Wt.
\end{array}
\begin{array}{ccccc}
BR & EP & RP & PD & CI \\
\left(3 \right. & 5 & 6 & 8 & \left. 4 \right)
\end{array}
\quad
\begin{array}{c}
 \\
BR \\
EP \\
RP \\
PD \\
CI
\end{array}
\begin{array}{ccccccc}
P & Ja & B & K & M & C & Jo \\
\left(9 \right. & 8 & 10 & 7 & 8 & 9 & 10 \\
10 & 9 & 9 & 10 & 10 & 9 & 10 \\
7 & 9 & 8 & 9 & 7 & 8 & 8 \\
9 & 10 & 9 & 8 & 10 & 8 & 9 \\
8 & 7 & 8 & 10 & 6 & 8 & \left. 7 \right)
\end{array}
$$

$$
= \begin{array}{ccccccc}
P & Ja & B & K & M & C & Jo \\
\left(223 \right. & 231 & 227 & 229 & 220 & 216 & \left. 228 \right)
\end{array}
$$

11. (a) Total cost for each opera troupe with each airline:

$$
\begin{array}{c}
P \\
E \\
AA
\end{array}
\begin{array}{ccc}
1st & C & Y \\
\left(630 \right. & 420 & 250 \\
650 & 350 & 275 \\
700 & 370 & \left. 150 \right)
\end{array}
\quad
\begin{array}{c}
Stars \\
Adults \\
Youth
\end{array}
\begin{array}{cc}
C & LT \\
\left(2 \right. & 3 \\
30 & 19 \\
5 & \left. 0 \right)
\end{array}
=
\begin{array}{c}
P \\
E \\
AA
\end{array}
\begin{array}{cc}
C & LT \\
\left(15110 \right. & 9870 \\
13175 & 8600 \\
13250 & \left. 9130 \right)
\end{array}
$$

(b) Right-multiply the result of part (a) by the discount matrix

$$
\left(\begin{array}{c} 0.7 \\ 1 \end{array} \right)
$$

to yield airline costs

$$
\begin{array}{c}
P \\
E \\
AA
\end{array}
\begin{array}{c}
Cost \\
\left(\begin{array}{c} 20447 \\ 17822.5 \\ 18405 \end{array} \right)
\end{array}.
$$

(c) The new cost matrix is

$$
\left(\begin{array}{ccc}
0.7 & 0 & 0 \\
0 & 0.8 & 0 \\
0 & 0 & 0.75
\end{array} \right)
\begin{array}{c}
P \\
E \\
AA
\end{array}
\begin{array}{ccc}
1st & C & Y \\
\left(630 \right. & 420 & 250 \\
650 & 350 & 275 \\
700 & 370 & \left. 150 \right)
\end{array}
=
\begin{array}{c}
P \\
E \\
AA
\end{array}
\begin{array}{ccc}
1st & C & Y \\
\left(441 \right. & 294 & 175 \\
520 & 280 & 220 \\
525 & 277.5 & \left. 112.5 \right)
\end{array}.
$$

12. The Sunday survey leads to the following matrix of probabilities:

$$
\begin{array}{c}
\phantom{<30000} \quad Duke \quad\quad L'ville \quad\quad n.c. \\
\begin{array}{c} <30000 \\ >30000 \end{array}
\begin{pmatrix}
125/561 & 205/561 & 231/561 \\
435/655 & 105/655 & 115/655
\end{pmatrix}
\end{array}
$$

The answer is estimated by the following matrix multiplication:

$$
\begin{array}{c}
\begin{array}{cc} <30000 & >30000 \end{array} \\
\begin{pmatrix} 276 & 302 \end{pmatrix}
\end{array}
\begin{array}{c}
\phantom{<30000} Duke \quad L'ville \quad n.c. \\
\begin{array}{c} <30000 \\ >30000 \end{array}
\begin{pmatrix}
0.223 & 0.365 & 0.412 \\
0.664 & 0.160 & 0.176
\end{pmatrix}
\end{array}
\approx
\begin{array}{c}
Duke \quad L'ville \quad n.c. \\
\begin{pmatrix} 262 & 149 & 167 \end{pmatrix}
\end{array}
$$

13. In this problem, some answers require exchanging the rows and columns of a matrix before performing matrix multiplication. The technical term for this is the *transpose* of a matrix. The transpose of matrix A, denoted A^T, is a matrix whose rows are the columns of A. In other words, row 1 of A^T is column 1 of A, row 2 of A^T is column 2 of A, and so on.

(a) We are looking for a matrix showing the hours of each type of labor by months:

$$
A^T D = \begin{array}{c}
 \quad Oct \quad\quad Nov \\
\begin{array}{c} Cutting \\ Sewing \\ Finishing \end{array}
\begin{pmatrix}
1300 & 1520 \\
1800 & 2092.5 \\
1240 & 1362.5
\end{pmatrix}
\end{array}
$$

(b) We want an item-by-plant matrix:

$$
AC^T = \begin{array}{c}
 \quad East \quad Central \quad West \\
\begin{array}{c} Panda \\ Kangaroo \\ Rabbit \end{array}
\begin{pmatrix}
15.99 & 14.46 & 18.60 \\
18.36 & 16.64 & 21.22 \\
11.70 & 10.60 & 13.61
\end{pmatrix}
\end{array}
$$

(c) We want the entry in the first row and first column of a matrix with the row label representing the month and the column label naming the plant. The result of part (b) is an item-by-plant matrix, so left-multiplying the result of part (b) by D^T will yield the desired information, a cost of \$36,366.

$$
D^T(AC^T) = \begin{array}{c}
 \quad East \quad\quad Central \quad\quad West \\
\begin{array}{c} Oct \\ Nov \end{array}
\begin{pmatrix}
36366 & 32924 & 42220 \\
41677.5 & 37735 & 48364.3
\end{pmatrix}
\end{array}
$$

(d) We want the result to be a matrix with the row label naming the plant and the column label indicating the type of labor.

$$
BA = \begin{array}{c}
 \quad Cutting \quad Sewing \quad Finishing \\
\begin{array}{c} East \\ Central \\ West \end{array}
\begin{pmatrix}
29.3 & 41 & 27 \\
27 & 35.5 & 21.5 \\
28 & 38.5 & 25.5
\end{pmatrix}
\end{array}
$$

(e) Examine the main diagonal of the product of the result of part (d) and the transpose of
C. The daily amount each plant pays its personnel is East—\$815.55, Central—\$636.40,
and West—\$894.45.

$$
(BA)C^T = \begin{array}{c} \\ East \\ Central \\ West \end{array}
\begin{array}{ccc} East & Central & West \\ \\ \end{array}
\left(\begin{array}{ccc}
815.55 & 738.30 & 946.62 \\
702.60 & 636.40 & 814.55 \\
770.70 & 697.80 & 894.45
\end{array} \right)
$$

Section 4.2 Class Practice

1.

$$
\left(\begin{array}{ccc}
0 & 1 & 0 \\
1 & 0 & 0 \\
0 & 0 & 1
\end{array} \right)
\left(\begin{array}{ccc}
2 & 1 & 0 \\
1 & 0 & 2 \\
0 & 1 & -1
\end{array} \right) =
\left(\begin{array}{ccc}
1 & 0 & 2 \\
2 & 1 & 0 \\
0 & 1 & -1
\end{array} \right)
$$

To interchange rows 1 and 3, left-multiply by

$$
\left(\begin{array}{ccc}
0 & 0 & 1 \\
0 & 1 & 0 \\
1 & 0 & 0
\end{array} \right).
$$

To interchange rows 2 and 3, left-multiply by

$$
\left(\begin{array}{ccc}
1 & 0 & 0 \\
0 & 0 & 1 \\
0 & 1 & 0
\end{array} \right).
$$

2.

$$
\left(\begin{array}{ccc}
k & 0 & 0 \\
0 & 1 & 0 \\
0 & 0 & 1
\end{array} \right)
\left(\begin{array}{ccc}
2 & 1 & 0 \\
1 & 0 & 2 \\
0 & 1 & -1
\end{array} \right) =
\left(\begin{array}{ccc}
2k & k & 0 \\
1 & 0 & 2 \\
0 & 1 & -1
\end{array} \right)
$$

To multiply row 2 by k, left-multiply by

$$
\left(\begin{array}{ccc}
1 & 0 & 0 \\
0 & k & 0 \\
0 & 0 & 1
\end{array} \right).
$$

To multiply row 3 by k, left-multiply by

$$
\left(\begin{array}{ccc}
1 & 0 & 0 \\
0 & 1 & 0 \\
0 & 0 & k
\end{array} \right).
$$

3.

$$\begin{pmatrix} 1 & k & 0 \\ 0 & 1 & 0 \\ 0 & 0 & 1 \end{pmatrix} \begin{pmatrix} 2 & 1 & 0 \\ 1 & 0 & 2 \\ 0 & 1 & -1 \end{pmatrix} = \begin{pmatrix} 2+k & 1 & 2k \\ 1 & 0 & 2 \\ 0 & 1 & -1 \end{pmatrix}$$

To add k times the third row to the first row, left-multiply by

$$\begin{pmatrix} 1 & 0 & k \\ 0 & 1 & 0 \\ 0 & 0 & 1 \end{pmatrix}.$$

To add k times the second row to the third row, left-multiply by

$$\begin{pmatrix} 1 & 0 & 0 \\ 0 & 1 & 0 \\ 0 & k & 1 \end{pmatrix}.$$

4. Interchange rows 1 and 2:

$$\begin{pmatrix} 0 & 1 & 0 \\ 1 & 0 & 0 \\ 0 & 0 & 1 \end{pmatrix}$$

Add -2 times row 1 to row 2:

$$\begin{pmatrix} 1 & 0 & 0 \\ -2 & 1 & 0 \\ 0 & 0 & 1 \end{pmatrix}$$

Add -1 times row 2 to row 3:

$$\begin{pmatrix} 1 & 0 & 0 \\ 0 & 1 & 0 \\ 0 & -1 & 1 \end{pmatrix}$$

Multiply row 3 by $\frac{1}{3}$:

$$\begin{pmatrix} 1 & 0 & 0 \\ 0 & 1 & 0 \\ 0 & 0 & \frac{1}{3} \end{pmatrix}$$

Add 4 times row 3 to row 2:

$$\begin{pmatrix} 1 & 0 & 0 \\ 0 & 1 & 4 \\ 0 & 0 & 1 \end{pmatrix}$$

Add -2 times row 3 to row 1:

$$\begin{pmatrix} 1 & 0 & -2 \\ 0 & 1 & 0 \\ 0 & 0 & 1 \end{pmatrix}$$

5. The result of the multiplication is the matrix shown on the left below, which is A^{-1}, as verified by multiplication with A.

$$\begin{pmatrix} 2/3 & -1/3 & -2/3 \\ -1/3 & 2/3 & 4/3 \\ -1/3 & 2/3 & 1/3 \end{pmatrix} \begin{pmatrix} 2 & 1 & 0 \\ 1 & 0 & 2 \\ 0 & 1 & -1 \end{pmatrix} = \begin{pmatrix} 1 & 0 & 0 \\ 0 & 1 & 0 \\ 0 & 0 & 1 \end{pmatrix}$$

6. The matrices must be left-multiplied, since matrix multiplication is not commutative. The order of multiplication corresponds to the sequence of EROs.

Section 4.4 Exercises

1. (a)

	Petr.	Text.	Tran.	Chem.
Petr.	0.1	0.4	0.6	0.2
Text.	0	0.1	0	0.1
Tran.	0.2	0.15	0.1	0.3
Chem.	0.4	0.3	0.25	0.2

(b) Petroleum is most dependent upon chemicals and least dependent upon textiles.

(c) $0.4(\$4,000,000) = \$1,600,000$

(d) The internal consumption matrix is

$$TP = \begin{array}{c} Petr. \\ Text. \\ Tran. \\ Chem. \end{array} \begin{pmatrix} 730 \\ 95 \\ 485 \\ 705 \end{pmatrix}.$$

Since 730 units of petroleum are used internally, 70 units of petroleum are left over for external use.

(e) The production matrix is

$$P = (I - T)^{-1}D = \begin{array}{c} Petr. \\ Text. \\ Tran. \\ Chem. \end{array} \begin{pmatrix} 195.6 \\ 39.3 \\ 154.4 \\ 213.3 \end{pmatrix}.$$

2. The new production matrix is

$$P$$
$$\begin{array}{c} Petr. \\ Text. \\ Tran. \\ Chem. \end{array} \begin{pmatrix} 391.11 \\ 78.5 \\ 308.83 \\ 426.5 \end{pmatrix},$$

which is double the original production matrix.

3.

$$
\begin{array}{cc}
 & P \\
\begin{array}{c} Manu. \\ Petr. \\ Tran. \\ HP \end{array} &
\begin{pmatrix} 579.25 \\ 572.31 \\ 476.21 \\ 464.83 \end{pmatrix}
\end{array}
$$

4. (a)

$$
\begin{array}{cccc}
 & Steel & Coal & Tran. \\
\begin{array}{c} Steel \\ Coal \\ Tran. \end{array} &
\begin{pmatrix} 0.2 & 0.20 & 0.35 \\ 0.3 & 0.19 & 0.15 \\ 0.15 & 0.23 & 0.1 \end{pmatrix}
\end{array}
$$

(b) Coal relies most on transportation; it relies least on itself.

(c) Transportation.

(d)

$$
P - TP =
\begin{array}{cc}
 & D \\
\begin{array}{c} Steel \\ Coal \\ Tran. \end{array} &
\begin{pmatrix} 4.55 \\ 10.98 \\ 5.51 \end{pmatrix}
\end{array}
$$

(e)

$$
P = (I - T)^{-1}D =
\begin{array}{cc}
 & P \\
\begin{array}{c} Steel \\ Coal \\ Tran. \end{array} &
\begin{pmatrix} 58.96 \\ 52.05 \\ 36.46 \end{pmatrix}
\end{array}
$$

Section 4.6 Exercises

1. There are no elementary row operations which can create a one in a column with all zeros; thus, such a matrix could never be transformed into an identity matrix.

2. (a) $x = 1$, $y = 1$, $z = 1$.

    (b) The system is dependent and has an infinite number of solutions.

    (c) The system is inconsistent and has no solutions.

3. (a)

$$
\begin{pmatrix} 0.16 & -0.04 & 0.24 \\ -0.07 & -0.07 & 0.07 \\ 0.04 & -0.08 & 0 \end{pmatrix}
$$

(b)

$$\begin{pmatrix} 10 & -20 & 15 & -4 \\ -7.83 & 19 & -15.5 & 4.3 \\ 2 & -5.5 & 5 & -1.5 \\ -0.17 & 0.5 & -0.5 & 0.17 \end{pmatrix}$$

4. The entire amount of $100,000 will go to the Hillsborough location.

5. (a) 4 hamburgers and 4 chicken sandwiches

   (b) 1/2 hamburger (which really means no hamburgers) and 8 chicken sandwiches

   (c) 7.5 hamburgers (so just 7 complete hamburgers) and 0 chicken sandwiches

6. The inverse of the given matrix is

$$\begin{pmatrix} \cos\theta & \sin\theta \\ -\sin\theta & \cos\theta \end{pmatrix}.$$

Multiplying this matrix on the right by

$$\begin{pmatrix} x \\ y \end{pmatrix}$$

rotates the point (x, y) through an angle θ in the clockwise direction—the opposite effect of the first matrix.

7. (a) The Student Council would receive $15,000, and the Beta Club would receive $22,500, but the 4-H Club would have to pay $7,500—an obvious problem with the solution.

   (b) The Beta Club would receive $30,000 and the other groups would receive nothing.

   (c) The Student Council receives $7,500, the Beta Club receives $11,250, and the 4-H Club receives $11,250.

Section 5.1 Class Practice

1. 52.14

2. 51.3252

Section 5.2 Class Practice

Both methods give equal answers to at least 4 decimal places using the *Matrix* software.

Section 5.3 Exercises

1. (a) The population distribution in five years is

$$
X_{20} = \begin{matrix} 0-3 \\ 3-6 \\ 6-9 \\ 9-12 \\ 12-15 \\ 15-18 \end{matrix} \begin{pmatrix} 27.4568 \\ 15.9868 \\ 13.9652 \\ 12.1983 \\ 9.46735 \\ 5.51225 \end{pmatrix},
$$

so the female population in the 6–9 bracket after 5 years is 13.9652, and the total population in this bracket is 27.9304.

(b) The population distribution in ten years is

$$
X_{40} = \begin{matrix} 0-3 \\ 3-6 \\ 6-9 \\ 9-12 \\ 12-15 \\ 15-18 \end{matrix} \begin{pmatrix} 50.0082 \\ 29.1188 \\ 25.4330 \\ 22.2137 \\ 17.2461 \\ 10.0421 \end{pmatrix},
$$

so the female population in the 6–9 bracket after 10 years is 25.433, for a total population in this bracket of 50.866.

2. There are 248.886 females after 56 quarters and 256.46 females after 57 quarters, so it takes 14–15 years for the total population to exceed 500.

3. (a) There are 243.934 females after 56 quarters and 251.357 females after 57 quarters.

   (b) There are 249.012 females after 66 quarters and 256.589 females after 67 quarters.

   (c) There are 246.026 females after 69 quarters and 253.513 females after 70 quarters.

4. (a) 3.0430%

   (b) 3.0428%

   (c) 3.0432%

It appears that the long-term growth rate is independent of the initial distribution.

5. For the first distribution, the female population in each bracket after 100 quarters is

$$
\begin{matrix} 0-3 \\ 3-6 \\ 6-9 \\ 9-12 \\ 12-15 \\ 15-18 \end{matrix} \begin{pmatrix} 365.977 \\ 213.101 \\ 186.127 \\ 162.567 \\ 126.213 \\ 73.4913 \end{pmatrix}.
$$

For the second distribution, the female population in each bracket after 100 quarters is

$$
\begin{array}{cc}
 & Pop. \\
\begin{array}{c}
0-3 \\
3-6 \\
6-9 \\
9-12 \\
12-15 \\
15-18
\end{array} &
\begin{pmatrix}
447.468 \\
278.020 \\
242.829 \\
212.091 \\
164.662 \\
95.8796
\end{pmatrix}
\end{array}.
$$

The proportion of the total population in each bracket after 100 quarters is

$$
\begin{array}{cc}
 & Prop. \\
\begin{array}{c}
0-3 \\
3-6 \\
6-9 \\
9-12 \\
12-15 \\
15-18
\end{array} &
\begin{pmatrix}
0.324597 \\
0.189007 \\
0.165082 \\
0.144186 \\
0.111942 \\
0.065200
\end{pmatrix}
\end{array}
$$

for the first distribution, and

$$
\begin{array}{cc}
 & Prop. \\
\begin{array}{c}
0-3 \\
3-6 \\
6-9 \\
9-12 \\
12-15 \\
15-18
\end{array} &
\begin{pmatrix}
0.324598 \\
0.189007 \\
0.165083 \\
0.144187 \\
0.111943 \\
0.065200
\end{pmatrix}
\end{array}
$$

for the second distribution. The long-term proportions of the population in each age group are independent of the initial distribution.

6. (a) 35 years

   (b)

$$
\begin{pmatrix}
0 & 0 & 1.2 & 0.8 & 0.7 & 0.2 & 0 \\
0.5 & 0 & 0 & 0 & 0 & 0 & 0 \\
0 & 0.8 & 0 & 0 & 0 & 0 & 0 \\
0 & 0 & 0.9 & 0 & 0 & 0 & 0 \\
0 & 0 & 0 & 0.9 & 0 & 0 & 0 \\
0 & 0 & 0 & 0 & 0.7 & 0 & 0 \\
0 & 0 & 0 & 0 & 0 & 0.5 & 0
\end{pmatrix}
$$

(c) The female age distribution after 300 years, or 60 cycles, is

$$
\begin{array}{c}
 \\
0-5 \\
5-10 \\
10-15 \\
15-20 \\
20-25 \\
25-30 \\
30-35
\end{array}
\overset{\textit{Pop.}}{
\begin{pmatrix}
110.651 \\
54.7612 \\
43.3620 \\
38.6276 \\
34.4102 \\
23.8414 \\
11.7991
\end{pmatrix}}
$$

The total female population is 317.453.

(d) After 305 years, the total female population is 320.725, so the growth rate is approximately 1.0307%.

(e) After 69.49 cycles, or about 350 years.

Section 5.5 Exercises

1. (a) After reaching the maximum sustainable population, remove 1.02% of the mammals from each age group during every 5-year cycle.

   (b) The new Leslie matrix L' is related to the original Leslie matrix L by $L' = \frac{1}{1+r}L$, or $L' = \frac{1}{1.010307}L$. After 69 cycles, the population distribution is

$$
\begin{array}{c}
 \\
0-5 \\
5-10 \\
10-15 \\
15-20 \\
20-25 \\
25-30 \\
30-35
\end{array}
\overset{\textit{Pop.}}{
\begin{pmatrix}
121.350 \\
60.0560 \\
47.5546 \\
42.3625 \\
37.7372 \\
26.1466 \\
12.9399
\end{pmatrix}},
$$

and after 89 cycles,

$$
\begin{array}{c}
 \\
0-5 \\
5-10 \\
10-15 \\
15-20 \\
20-25 \\
25-30 \\
30-35
\end{array}
\overset{\textit{Pop.}}{
\begin{pmatrix}
121.351 \\
60.0567 \\
47.5552 \\
42.3630 \\
37.7377 \\
26.1469 \\
12.9400
\end{pmatrix}}.
$$

The population is stable.

2. (a) The total female population under 50 years old (in thousands) after 15 cycles is 2143.83; after 16 cycles, 2307.39; after 17 cycles, 2483.5; and after 18 cycles, 2672.86. The growth rates for these cycles are 7.629%, 7.632%, and 7.625%. The long-term growth rate is therefore about 7.63%.

   (b) The net reproductive rate is $R = 1.49611$, so the birth rates must be reduced by an amount $b = 0.3316$.

   (c) The new Leslie matrix has the approximate entries

$$\begin{pmatrix} 0 & 0.0002 & 0.0392 & 0.1912 & 0.2994 & 0.2433 & 0.1488 & 0.0699 & 0.019 & 0.002 \\ 0.9965 & 0 & 0 & 0 & 0 & 0 & 0 & 0 & 0 & 0 \\ 0 & 0.9982 & 0 & 0 & 0 & 0 & 0 & 0 & 0 & 0 \\ 0 & 0 & 0.998 & 0 & 0 & 0 & 0 & 0 & 0 & 0 \\ 0 & 0 & 0 & 0.9979 & 0 & 0 & 0 & 0 & 0 & 0 \\ 0 & 0 & 0 & 0 & 0.9969 & 0 & 0 & 0 & 0 & 0 \\ 0 & 0 & 0 & 0 & 0 & 0.9962 & 0 & 0 & 0 & 0 \\ 0 & 0 & 0 & 0 & 0 & 0 & 0.9946 & 0 & 0 & 0 \\ 0 & 0 & 0 & 0 & 0 & 0 & 0 & 0.9918 & 0 & 0 \\ 0 & 0 & 0 & 0 & 0 & 0 & 0 & 0 & 0.987 & 0 \end{pmatrix}.$$

   The female population under 50 years old stabilizes near 818,000 after about 100 years (20 cycles).

3. (a) The long-term growth rate is 17.56%.

   (b) The harvesting coefficient h is approximately 0.15. The uniform harvesting policy is to remove 15% of the sheep from each of the 12 age classes every year.

   (c) The percentage distribution after harvesting begins is given by the vector

	Percent
$0-1$	24.1
$1-2$	17.3
$2-3$	14.4
$3-4$	11.8
$4-5$	9.5
$5-6$	7.5
$6-7$	5.7
$7-8$	4.1
$8-9$	2.8
$9-10$	1.6
$10-11$	0.8
$11-12$	0.2

Section 6.0 Class Practice

1. (a) 0.4; 0.

(b) 0.2

2. The stable state vector for the taxi problem is

$$\begin{array}{ccc} N & D & S \\ \left(0.3 & 0.3 & 0.4\right). \end{array}$$

The stable state vector does not depend upon the initial distribution. The entries in the stable state vector are the probabilities of being in each state over the long run no matter what state is the starting state. Different initial distributions may affect the amount of time required to converge to the stable distribution; nevertheless, all initial distributions will eventually lead to the stable state vector.

Section 6.1 Exercises

1. (a)

$$\begin{array}{c} \\ 1 \\ 2 \\ 3 \\ 4 \\ 5 \end{array} \begin{array}{ccccc} 1 & 2 & 3 & 4 & 5 \\ \left(\begin{array}{ccccc} 0 & \frac{1}{2} & 0 & 0 & \frac{1}{2} \\ \frac{1}{2} & 0 & 0 & 0 & \frac{1}{2} \\ 0 & 0 & 0 & 1 & 0 \\ 0 & 0 & \frac{1}{2} & 0 & \frac{1}{2} \\ \frac{1}{3} & \frac{1}{3} & 0 & \frac{1}{3} & 0 \end{array}\right) \end{array}$$

(b) 0; 0.083.

(c) The stable state vector is

$$\begin{array}{ccccc} 1 & 2 & 3 & 4 & 5 \\ \left(0.2 & 0.2 & 0.1 & 0.2 & 0.3\right). \end{array}$$

(d) The long-run probability of being in room 4 is 0.2.

(e) In the long run, the rat will spend 30% of the time in rooms 2 or 3.

2. (a)

$$\begin{array}{c} \\ 0 \\ 1 \\ 2 \\ 3 \end{array} \begin{array}{cccc} 0 & 1 & 2 & 3 \\ \left(\begin{array}{cccc} 1/4 & 3/4 & 0 & 0 \\ 1/6 & 1/2 & 1/3 & 0 \\ 0 & 1/2 & 5/12 & 1/12 \\ 0 & 0 & 1 & 0 \end{array}\right) \end{array}$$

(b) Starting in state 3 (all red in jar A), the probability that there will be 2 red beads in jar A after 3 transitions is 0.4236.

(c) The probability that there will be 2 red beads in jar A in the long run is 0.343.

3. (a)

$$\begin{array}{c} \\ W \\ D \\ A \end{array} \begin{array}{ccc} W & D & A \\ \begin{pmatrix} 0 & 1 & 0 \\ 0 & 0 & 1 \\ 0.5 & 0.5 & 0 \end{pmatrix} \end{array}$$

(b)

$$P^2 = \begin{pmatrix} 0 & 0 & 1 \\ 0.5 & 0.5 & 0 \\ 0 & 0.5 & 0.5 \end{pmatrix} \qquad P^4 = \begin{pmatrix} 0 & 0.5 & 0.5 \\ 0.25 & 0.25 & 0.5 \\ 0.25 & 0.5 & 0.25 \end{pmatrix}$$

$$P^6 = \begin{pmatrix} 0.25 & 0.5 & 0.25 \\ 0.125 & 0.375 & 0.5 \\ 0.25 & 0.375 & 0.375 \end{pmatrix} \qquad P^{10} = \begin{pmatrix} 0.1875 & 0.375 & 0.4375 \\ 0.21875 & 0.40625 & 0.375 \\ 0.1875 & 0.40625 & 0.40625 \end{pmatrix}$$

The zero entries vanish because by the sixth throw everyone has a chance to catch the frisbee no matter who has it initially.

4. (a)

$$\begin{array}{c} \\ OR \\ FF \\ CC \end{array} \begin{array}{ccc} OR & FF & CC \\ \begin{pmatrix} 0.5 & 0.35 & 0.15 \\ 0.3 & 0.4 & 0.3 \\ 0.2 & 0.55 & 0.25 \end{pmatrix} \end{array}$$

(b) The manager should expect to sell $40(0.35) + 30(0.4) + 25(0.55) = 39.75$, which rounds to 40 orders of french fries.

(c) Assuming 5 days in a week, this will involve 10 transitions.

$$\begin{pmatrix} 40 & 30 & 25 \end{pmatrix} T^{10} = \begin{pmatrix} 32.8 & 39.7 & 22.45 \end{pmatrix}$$

The manager will sell 33 orders of onion rings, 40 orders of fries, and 22 cookies.

(d) Assume 180 school days in the year.

$$\begin{pmatrix} 40 & 30 & 25 \end{pmatrix} T^{180} = \begin{pmatrix} 32.82 & 39.73 & 22.45 \end{pmatrix}$$

The manager will sell 33 orders of onion rings, 40 orders of fries, and 22 cookies each day.

(e) The rows of the powers of the transition matrix converge to values that indicate that onion rings will be ordered 34.5% of the time, french fries will be ordered 41.8% of the time, and cookies will be ordered 23.6% of the time.

5. (a) Yes; the stable state vector is

$$\begin{pmatrix} 0.2825 & 0.3455 & 0.1900 & 0.1822 \end{pmatrix}.$$

(b) The stable state vector shows that 18.22% of the students buy ice cream. A Markov Chain model assumes that each step in the process depends only on what happened in the previous step, so it is assumed that people who had ice cream more than 1 day before forgot that they did not like it.

(c) A Markov chain is not a good model for the situation. People will remember that they do not like the ice cream, so what they buy each day is dependent on more than what they bought the day before.

6. (a)

$$
\begin{array}{c c c c c c c c c c}
 & 1 & 2 & 3 & 4 & 5 & 6 & 7 & 8 & 9 \\
1 & 1 & 0 & 0 & 0 & 0 & 0 & 0 & 0 & 0 \\
2 & 1/6 & 1/6 & 1/3 & 1/3 & 0 & 0 & 0 & 0 & 0 \\
3 & 0 & 1/2 & 1/2 & 0 & 0 & 0 & 0 & 0 & 0 \\
4 & 0 & 1/2 & 0 & 1/4 & 1/4 & 0 & 0 & 0 & 0 \\
5 & 1/5 & 0 & 0 & 1/5 & 1/5 & 2/5 & 0 & 0 & 0 \\
6 & 0 & 0 & 0 & 0 & 1/3 & 1/6 & 1/3 & 1/6 & 0 \\
7 & 0 & 0 & 0 & 0 & 0 & 0 & 1 & 0 & 0 \\
8 & 0 & 0 & 0 & 1/5 & 0 & 1/5 & 0 & 1/5 & 2/5 \\
9 & 0 & 0 & 0 & 0 & 0 & 0 & 0 & 2/3 & 1/3 \\
\end{array}
$$

(b) 0.7757

(c) Starting in room 6 offers the highest probability (0.6355) of ending in Room 7. Starting in either room 2 or 3 offers the same low probability (0.1495) of ending in Room 7.

7. (a)

$$
\begin{array}{c c c c c}
 & I & II & III & IV \\
I & 1 & 0 & 0 & 0 \\
II & 0 & 1 & 0 & 0 \\
III & 0 & 0.01994 & 0.98 & 0.00006 \\
IV & 0.02 & 0.03 & 0 & 0.95 \\
\end{array}
$$

(b)

$$
\begin{array}{c c c c c}
 & I & II & III & IV \\
I & 1 & 0 & 0 & 0 \\
II & 0 & 1 & 0 & 0 \\
III & 0.0012 & 0.9988 & 0 & 0 \\
IV & 0.4 & 0.6 & 0 & 0 \\
\end{array}
$$

(c) 0.0012

8. The transition matrix for this Markov chain is

$$
\begin{array}{c c c c}
 & Prof. & Serv. & Manu. \\
Prof. & 0.63 & 0.20 & 0.17 \\
Serv. & 0.31 & 0.45 & 0.24 \\
Manu. & 0.41 & 0.41 & 0.18 \\
\end{array}
$$

(a) 0.3335

(b)

$$\begin{pmatrix} 0.41 & 0.27 & 0.32 \end{pmatrix} T^{10} = \begin{pmatrix} 0.484 & 0.321 & 0.194 \end{pmatrix}$$

In ten generations, 48% will be professionals.

9. The sequence of elected presidents since 1900, with party affiliation, is as follows: T. Roosevelt (R), Taft (R), Wilson (D), Harding (R), Coolidge (R), Hoover (R), F. D. Roosevelt (D), Truman (D), Eisenhower (R), Kennedy (D), Johnson (D), Nixon (R), Carter (D), Reagan (R). The transition matrix for the Markov chain model is

$$\begin{array}{cc} & \begin{array}{cc} Rep. & Dem. \end{array} \\ \begin{array}{c} Rep. \\ Dem. \end{array} & \begin{pmatrix} 7/11 & 4/11 \\ 4/10 & 6/10 \end{pmatrix}. \end{array}$$

In 1988, the probability is 7/11 that a Republican will be elected. In the year 2001, the probability is about 0.525 that our president will be Republican. The main weakness of this model is the assumption that voters will not remember previous presidents.

10. (a)

$$\begin{array}{c} \begin{array}{c} Well \\ Ill \\ Immune \\ Dead \end{array} \begin{array}{cccc} Well & Ill & Immune & Dead \\ \begin{pmatrix} 0.80 & 0.20 & 0 & 0 \\ 0 & 0.55 & 0.40 & 0.05 \\ 0 & 0 & 1 & 0 \\ 0 & 0 & 0 & 1 \end{pmatrix} \end{array} \end{array}$$

(b) (i) 0.7189 (ii) 0.8028 (iii) 0.7751 (iv) 0.8866

(c) The Markov chain does not have a stable state because of the absorbing states; however, the transition matrix raised to a large power does stabilize as

$$\begin{array}{c} \begin{array}{c} Well \\ Ill \\ Immune \\ Dead \end{array} \begin{array}{cccc} Well & Ill & Immune & Dead \\ \begin{pmatrix} 0 & 0 & 0.8889 & 0.1111 \\ 0 & 0 & 0.8889 & 0.1111 \\ 0 & 0 & 1 & 0 \\ 0 & 0 & 0 & 1 \end{pmatrix}. \end{array} \end{array}$$

11. The transition matrix is

	1	2	3	4	5	6	7	8	9
1	0	0.2	0.5	0.2	0.1	0	0	0	0
2	0.35	0	0	0.5	0	0.15	0	0	0
3	0.2	0.3	0	0	0.3	0	0.2	0	0
4	0.4	0.25	0	0	0	0.25	0	0.1	0
5	0.1	0.1	0.4	0	0	0	0.35	0	0.05
6	0.25	0.1	0.2	0.25	0	0	0	0.2	0
7	0.1	0.05	0.2	0	0.5	0	0	0	0.15
8	0	0	0	0	0	0	0	1	0
9	0	0	0	0	0	0	0	0	1

Raising the transition matrix to a large power and looking at the entry in row 1 and column 9, the probability that Duke will score is about 0.40.

12. The transition matrix is

$$
\begin{array}{c c}
 & \begin{array}{cccc} A & B & C & D \end{array} \\
\begin{array}{c} A \\ B \\ C \\ D \end{array} &
\left(\begin{array}{cccc}
0 & 1/2 & 0 & 1/2 \\
1/3 & 0 & 2/3 & 0 \\
0 & 1/3 & 0 & 2/3 \\
1/4 & 0 & 3/4 & 0
\end{array}\right).
\end{array}
$$

(a) For example, notice that

$$
A^7 =
\begin{array}{c c}
 & \begin{array}{cccc} A & B & C & D \end{array} \\
\begin{array}{c} A \\ B \\ C \\ D \end{array} &
\left(\begin{array}{cccc}
0 & 0.38 & 0 & 0.62 \\
0.28 & 0 & 0.72 & 0 \\
0 & 0.38 & 0 & 0.62 \\
0.28 & 0 & 0.72 & 0
\end{array}\right)
\end{array}
$$

and

$$
A^8 =
\begin{array}{c c}
 & \begin{array}{cccc} A & B & C & D \end{array} \\
\begin{array}{c} A \\ B \\ C \\ D \end{array} &
\left(\begin{array}{cccc}
0.28 & 0 & 0.72 & 0 \\
0 & 0.38 & 0 & 0.62 \\
0.28 & 0 & 0.72 & 0 \\
0 & 0.38 & 0 & 0.62
\end{array}\right).
\end{array}
$$

(b) The entries in the transition matrix should be halved to account for the oscillating pattern. The ant will spend 14% of the time at A, 19% of the time at B, 36% of the time at C, and 31% of the time at D.

Section 7.3 Exercises

1. The transformation is performed by the matrix multiplication

$$
\begin{pmatrix}
1 & 0 & 0 \\
0 & -1 & 0 \\
0 & 0 & 1
\end{pmatrix}
\begin{pmatrix}
2 & 1.5 & 3 \\
1 & 2 & 4 \\
1 & 1 & 1
\end{pmatrix}
=
\begin{pmatrix}
2 & 1.5 & 3 \\
-1 & -2 & -4 \\
1 & 1 & 1
\end{pmatrix}.
$$

The transformed points have coordinates $(2, -1)$, $(1.5, -2)$, and $(3, -4)$.

2. The transformation is performed by the matrix multiplication

$$
\begin{pmatrix}
-1 & 0 & 0 \\
0 & 1 & 0 \\
0 & 0 & 1
\end{pmatrix}
\begin{pmatrix}
2 & 1.5 & 3 \\
1 & 2 & 4 \\
1 & 1 & 1
\end{pmatrix}
=
\begin{pmatrix}
-2 & -1.5 & -3 \\
1 & 2 & 4 \\
1 & 1 & 1
\end{pmatrix}.
$$

The transformed points have coordinates $(-2, 1)$, $(-1.5, 2)$, and $(-3, 4)$.

3. The transformation is performed by the matrix multiplication

$$\begin{pmatrix} 1 & 0 & -3 \\ 0 & 1 & -2 \\ 0 & 0 & 1 \end{pmatrix} \begin{pmatrix} \cos 75° & -\sin 75° & 0 \\ \sin 75° & \cos 75° & 0 \\ 0 & 0 & 1 \end{pmatrix} \begin{pmatrix} 1 & 0 & 0 \\ 0 & 1 & 0 \\ 0 & 0 & 1/3 \end{pmatrix} \begin{pmatrix} 2 & 1.5 & 3 \\ 1 & 2 & 4 \\ 1 & 1 & 1 \end{pmatrix}$$

$$= \begin{pmatrix} -1.45 & -2.54 & -4.09 \\ 1.52 & 1.30 & 3.27 \\ 0.33 & 0.33 & 0.33 \end{pmatrix}.$$

The transformed points have coordinates $(-4.34, 4.57)$, $(-7.63, 3.90)$, and $(-12.26, 9.80)$.

4. The transformation is performed by the matrix multiplication

$$\begin{pmatrix} 1 & 0 & 0 \\ 0 & 1 & 0 \\ 0 & 0 & 2 \end{pmatrix} \begin{pmatrix} \cos(-45°) & -\sin(-45°) & 0 \\ \sin(-45°) & \cos(-45°) & 0 \\ 0 & 0 & 1 \end{pmatrix} \begin{pmatrix} 1 & 0 & -2 \\ 0 & 1 & -1 \\ 0 & 0 & 1 \end{pmatrix} \begin{pmatrix} 2 & 1.5 & 3 \\ 1 & 2 & 4 \\ 1 & 1 & 1 \end{pmatrix}$$

$$= \begin{pmatrix} 0 & 0.35 & 2.83 \\ 0 & 1.06 & 1.41 \\ 2 & 2 & 2 \end{pmatrix}.$$

The transformed points have coordinates $(0,0)$, $(0.18, 0.53)$, and $(1.42, 0.71)$.

Section 7.5 Exercises

1.

$$\begin{pmatrix} 1 & 0 & 0 & 0 \\ 0 & -1 & 0 & 0 \\ 0 & 0 & 1 & 0 \\ 0 & 0 & 0 & 1 \end{pmatrix}$$

2.

$$\begin{pmatrix} 0 & 0 & 0 & 0 \\ 0 & 1 & 0 & 0 \\ 0 & 0 & 1 & 0 \\ -1/10 & 0 & 0 & 1 \end{pmatrix}$$

3. Multiply the following matrices:

$$\begin{pmatrix} 1 & 0 & 0 & 0 \\ 0 & \cos 45° & -\sin 45° & 0 \\ 0 & \sin 45° & \cos 45° & 0 \\ 0 & 0 & 0 & 1 \end{pmatrix} \begin{pmatrix} \cos 20° & -\sin 20° & 0 & 0 \\ \sin 20° & \cos 20° & 0 & 0 \\ 0 & 0 & 1 & 0 \\ 0 & 0 & 0 & 1 \end{pmatrix}$$

4. Multiply the following matrices:

$$
\begin{pmatrix}
0 & 0 & 0 & 0 \\
0 & 1 & 0 & 0 \\
0 & 0 & 1 & 0 \\
-1/5 & 0 & 0 & 1
\end{pmatrix}
\begin{pmatrix}
1 & 0 & 0 & 1 \\
0 & 1 & 0 & 2 \\
0 & 0 & 1 & -1 \\
0 & 0 & 0 & 1
\end{pmatrix}
\begin{pmatrix}
1 & 0 & 0 & 0 \\
0 & 1 & 0 & 0 \\
0 & 0 & 1 & 0 \\
0 & 0 & 0 & 1/2
\end{pmatrix}
$$

5. First rotate parallel to the xy-plane by an angle $-45°$, which moves the observer to the xz-plane. Next rotate in the xz-plane by an angle $\theta = -\tan^{-1}(1/\sqrt{2})$, which moves the observer to the x-axis at a distance $10\sqrt{3}$ from the origin. The entire transformation is accomplished by multiplying the following matrices:

$$
\begin{pmatrix}
0 & 0 & 0 & 0 \\
0 & 1 & 0 & 0 \\
0 & 0 & 1 & 0 \\
-1/10\sqrt{3} & 0 & 0 & 1
\end{pmatrix}
\begin{pmatrix}
\cos\theta & 0 & -\sin\theta & 1 \\
0 & 1 & 0 & 0 \\
\sin\theta & 0 & \cos\theta & 0 \\
0 & 0 & 0 & 1
\end{pmatrix}
\begin{pmatrix}
\cos(-45°) & -\sin(-45°) & 0 & 0 \\
\sin(-45°) & \cos(-45°) & 0 & 0 \\
0 & 0 & 1 & 0 \\
0 & 0 & 0 & 1
\end{pmatrix}
$$

6. Expressing the corners of the cube in homogeneous coordinates and multiplying by the matrix from Exercise 2 yields the result

$$
\begin{pmatrix}
0 & 0 & 0 & 0 \\
0 & 1 & 0 & 0 \\
0 & 0 & 1 & 0 \\
-1/10 & 0 & 0 & 1
\end{pmatrix}
\begin{pmatrix}
0 & 5 & 0 & 0 & 5 & 5 & 0 & 5 \\
0 & 0 & 5 & 0 & 5 & 0 & 5 & 5 \\
0 & 0 & 0 & 5 & 0 & 5 & 5 & 5 \\
1 & 1 & 1 & 1 & 1 & 1 & 1 & 1
\end{pmatrix}
=
\begin{pmatrix}
0 & 0 & 0 & 0 & 0 & 0 & 0 & 0 \\
0 & 0 & 5 & 0 & 5 & 0 & 5 & 5 \\
0 & 0 & 0 & 5 & 0 & 5 & 5 & 5 \\
1 & 0.5 & 1 & 1 & 0.5 & 0.5 & 1 & 0.5
\end{pmatrix}.
$$

The transformed coordinates in 3-space of the corners of the cube are $(0,0,0)$, $(0,0,0)$, $(0,5,0)$, $(0,0,5)$, $(0,10,0)$, $(0,0,10)$, $(0,5,5)$, and $(0,10,10)$. A picture of the cube as viewed from the point $(10,0,0)$ is shown below.

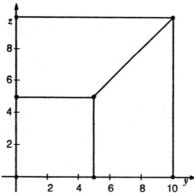

7. The observer is shifted from the point $(10,4,6)$ to a point on the x-axis by a rotation of $\theta_1 = -\tan^{-1}(2/5)$ parallel to the xy-plane followed by a rotation of $\theta_2 = -\tan^{-1}(6/\sqrt{116})$ in the xz-plane. After these rotations, the observer will be on the x-axis at a distance $\sqrt{152}$ units from the origin. The rotations and subsequent projection onto the yz-plane are performed by left-multiplying the matrix of homogeneous coordinates of the corners of the cube by the

following matrices:

$$\begin{pmatrix} 0 & 0 & 0 & 0 \\ 0 & 1 & 0 & 0 \\ 0 & 0 & 1 & 0 \\ -1/\sqrt{152} & 0 & 0 & 1 \end{pmatrix} \begin{pmatrix} \cos\theta_2 & 0 & -\sin\theta_2 & 0 \\ 0 & 1 & 0 & 0 \\ \sin\theta_2 & 0 & \cos\theta_2 & 0 \\ 0 & 0 & 0 & 1 \end{pmatrix} \begin{pmatrix} \cos\theta_1 & -\sin\theta_1 & 0 & 0 \\ \sin\theta_1 & \cos\theta_1 & 0 & 0 \\ 0 & 0 & 1 & 0 \\ 0 & 0 & 0 & 1 \end{pmatrix}$$

The homogeneous coordinates resulting from the multiplication above are

$$\begin{pmatrix} 0 & 0 & 0 & 0 & 0 & 0 & 0 & 0 \\ 0 & -1.86 & 4.64 & 0 & 2.79 & -1.86 & 4.64 & 2.79 \\ 0 & -2.26 & -0.90 & 4.37 & -3.16 & 2.11 & 3.46 & 1.20 \\ 1 & 0.67 & 0.87 & 0.80 & 0.54 & 0.47 & 0.67 & 0.34 \end{pmatrix}.$$

The transformed coordinates of the corners of the cube are

$$(0,0,0), \quad (0,-2.78,-3.37), \quad (0,5.33,-1.03), \quad (0,0,5.46), \quad (0,5.17,-5.85),$$

$$(0,-3.96,4.49), \quad (0,6.93,5.16), \quad \text{and} \quad (0,8.21,3.53).$$

The transformed corners are plotted in the coordinate system below, and the view of the cube from $(10,4,6)$ is shown.

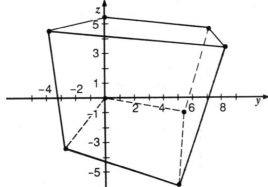

8. The observer is shifted from the point $(10,7,8)$ to a point on the x-axis by a rotation of $\theta_1 = -\tan^{-1}(7/10)$ parallel to the xy-plane followed by a rotation of $\theta_2 = -\tan^{-1}(8/\sqrt{149})$ in the xz-plane. After these rotations, the observer will be on the x-axis at a distance $\sqrt{213}$ units from the origin. The rotations and subsequent projection onto the yz-plane are performed by left-multiplying the matrix of homogeneous coordinates of the corners of the cube by the following matrices:

$$\begin{pmatrix} 0 & 0 & 0 & 0 \\ 0 & 1 & 0 & 0 \\ 0 & 0 & 1 & 0 \\ -1/\sqrt{213} & 0 & 0 & 1 \end{pmatrix} \begin{pmatrix} \cos\theta_2 & 0 & -\sin\theta_2 & 0 \\ 0 & 1 & 0 & 0 \\ \sin\theta_2 & 0 & \cos\theta_2 & 0 \\ 0 & 0 & 0 & 1 \end{pmatrix} \begin{pmatrix} \cos\theta_1 & -\sin\theta_1 & 0 & 0 \\ \sin\theta_1 & \cos\theta_1 & 0 & 0 \\ 0 & 0 & 1 & 0 \\ 0 & 0 & 0 & 1 \end{pmatrix}$$

The homogeneous coordinates resulting from the multiplication above are

$$\begin{pmatrix} 0 & 0 & 0 & 0 & 0 & 0 & 0 & 0 \\ 0 & -2.87 & 4.10 & 0 & 1.23 & -2.87 & 4.10 & 1.23 \\ 0 & -2.25 & -1.57 & 4.18 & -3.82 & 1.94 & 2.61 & 0.36 \\ 1 & 0.77 & 0.84 & 0.81 & 0.60 & 0.58 & 0.65 & 0.41 \end{pmatrix}.$$

The transformed coordinates of the corners of the cube are

$$(0,0,0), \quad (0,-3.73,-2.92), \quad (0,4.88,-1.87), \quad (0,0,5.16), \quad (0,2.05,-6.37),$$

$$(0,-4.95,3.34), \quad (0,6.31,4.02), \quad \text{and} \quad (0,3.00,0.88).$$

The transformed corners are plotted in the coordinate system below, and the view of the cube from $(10,7,8)$ is shown.

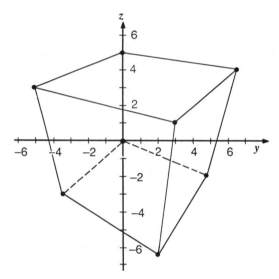

User's Guide for Matrix Software

The *Matrix* software, designed to accompany this *Matrices* unit, was developed by the Department of Mathematics and Computer Science at the North Carolina School of Science and Mathematics as part of its fourth-year high school mathematics course. The software runs on an IBM PC or compatible microcomputer with 512K memory. The software can be used by students on an individual basis and is also useful for demonstrations by a teacher in front of a class.

The software is menu-driven, meaning that menus appear on the screen with options for the user to choose from. The purpose of this guide is to assist you in choosing options and interpreting screens.

This guide is not intended to be comprehensive, but rather is designed to provide instruction in the basic tasks that most users would want to accomplish. The software offers a myriad of other possibilities; these are best explored independently after some basic techniques have been mastered.

The guide will be most useful if consulted while you are actively engaged in using the software.

8   General Information

Before you begin to use the software, it will be useful to read the following background information.

- The *Matrix* diskette contains files with the following suffixes: .EXE, .COM, .DES, .DOC, .BAT. These files contain the programs that run the computer. They occupy most of the space on the *Matrix* disk, leaving only 96256 bytes free.

- The software is designed to perform calculations using matrices. You will need to supply the matrices. Although there is some space on the disk, you will probably need a separate formatted disk on which to store files of matrices.

- Matrices that will be used several times or at different sessions on the computer should be stored on a data diskette. Files that contain a group of matrices should be given filenames that are at most 8 characters long and begin with a letter; the computer will automatically add the suffix .MAT to the names of files of matrices. You do not need to type the .MAT suffix when naming or requesting files. Matrices that are stored on disk can be retrieved for later use, even after exiting and reentering the program.

- During a single session, at most 50 matrices can be kept in memory for recall anytime during that session. Defining all 50, however, would leave no space for the matrix results of calculations. Note that once the program is exited, these matrices are lost unless they have been saved to a file on a diskette.

- Each matrix used with this software carries its dimension, an optional description, its entries, and a name while kept in memory during a single session or when saved on a file to a data disk. The matrix is recalled for use in the program by using the name given to it when defined.

• Entries of each matrix are shown accurate to the nearest hundredth. The level of accuracy of the display of matrix entries can be changed. However, there is no prompt for this action. The change in display can be accomplished when a matrix is displayed with the message $\boxed{\text{Press <RETURN> to Continue.}}$ at the bottom of the screen. At this point do not press Return, but instead press the period or decimal key (.). Type Y at the question $\boxed{\text{Change Matrix Screen Format(Y/N)?}}$. Now you have the option of selecting from 0 to 9 decimal places. Your choice of the number of decimal places will carry through the use of the software in this session unless you go through this procedure again to change the number of decimal places. When the program is exited and reentered, the number of decimals will go back to the default of 2 places.

• The software is menu-driven. When using the software, you will be asked to type in replies specifying your choice of action. All typed replies of more than one character must be followed by pressing Return. At any point in the software, you can return to the previous menu by typing Q. However, when Q is used, the current procedure is not completed, and any results of that procedure not already saved will be lost.

• When using the software, you will see several screens that provide some important information and the message $\boxed{\text{Press RETURN To Continue.}}$. Since the instruction from these screens is obvious (press Return), this manual will not make references to such screens.

• The software automatically enters all letters in uppercase. If the shift key is pressed with a letter, the letter will be lowercase. All parameters are shown as lowercase letters. Names of matrices are expected to be written using uppercase letters.

9   Getting Started

• To begin, insert the *Matrix* diskette into drive A, turn on the computer, and wait. The *Matrix* diskette will boot itself up in about a minute. As it is booting, you will see the expression **A>matrix.exe** on the screen. This indicates that the booting process is in progress. Once the software has loaded itself into memory, the NCSSM logo will appear. In another 15 seconds, the logo will disappear and the title page will be seen. The *Matrix* program is now ready to use.

• Pressing the F1 key at this point will give more information about this and other software that accompanies the Introduction to College Mathematics course for which the *Matrix* software was developed. The function keys (F-keys) are located at the left of the keyboard on an IBM PC. Pressing any key other than F1 will cause the main menu to be displayed. We will be primarily concerned with the first and fourth items on the main menu. The last two menu items (F5 and F6) offer somewhat specialized options for managing files and disk space.

10   Defining Matrices

The software is equipped to perform operations using matrices, but the user must supply the matrices and the appropriate operations. The first step, then, in using this software is to create matrices.

• At the main menu, the F10 menu, press F1 to select ⎢Define/Edit Matrix⎢. A new menu, the F1 menu, will appear. The most important options are 1, 2, 4, and 5. These options enable you to define four types of matrices: static, dynamic, identity, and constant. (A static matrix is a matrix with numerical entries, in contrast to a dynamic matrix that is defined in terms of operations between already defined matrices.) On this same menu you will be able to edit entries of a matrix. Remember, typing Q at any point will return you to the previous menu.

How to Define a Static Matrix

• At the F1 menu, type 1 indicating you wish to define a static matrix.

• You will first have to input the dimension of your matrix—the number of rows and then the number of columns. Both dimensions go on the same line with either a comma or a space between the number of rows and the number of columns. For example, you would type 3,2 to specify a matrix with three rows and two columns. The number of rows and columns must be integer values that range from 1 to 15.

• Next you will be asked for a verbal description of your matrix. The description, which is optional, must be 30 characters or less in length. Simply press Return at this prompt if you wish to omit a description. A description is useful if you plan to save a group of matrices, and the name alone is not sufficient to remind you of the significance of an individual matrix.

• Next you will be asked for the entries of the matrix by rows. These entries must be numerical and cannot include operations or functions. (Keep your calculator close by.) For example, if you want to show sin(40°) as an entry, you must input a decimal value of approximately 0.6428. Entries in a row should be separated by spaces or commas, and Return should be pressed at the completion of each row. If you type an insufficient number of entries, an error message will appear and you will have to repeat the entries for that row.

After entering all of the rows, the matrix you have defined will be displayed. Depending on the number of digits shown in each entry, the screen will show at least the first two columns and at most the first ten columns of your matrix. The arrow keys can be used to review the complete matrix if some columns are off the display. The columns and rows are labeled with numbers.

• If you wish to change the level of accuracy of the display of entries, you may do this when the message ⎢Press <RETURN> to Continue.⎢ appears on the screen. At this point press the period or decimal key (.). Type Y at the question ⎢Change Matrix Screen Format(Y/N)?⎢. Now you have the option of selecting from 0 to 9 decimal places. Your choice of the number of decimal places will remain throughout the use of the software in this session unless you go through this procedure again to change the number of decimal places. When the program is exited and then reentered, the number of decimals will return to the default of 2 places.

• If you press return at ⎢Press <RETURN> to Continue.⎢, the name of the matrix you have defined will be requested. The name must be no more than 8 characters and have no spaces, commas, periods, or symbols. Numbers may be included in the names of matrices. If no name is given, the matrix will be discarded from memory. You are then given the option to define another matrix. A Y for yes takes you back through the steps above, and an N takes you back to the F1 menu.

How to Define a Dynamic Matrix

A dynamic matrix is defined in terms of other already defined matrices. For example, suppose MAT1 is a 3×2 static matrix that you have already defined, and you need $(MAT1)^2$ in your computations. A dynamic matrix can be defined that is equal to matrix $(MAT1)^2$.

- To define a dynamic matrix, type 2 at the F1 menu.

- You will first be asked the name of the new dynamic matrix. After entering the name, you will be asked for a matrix definition. This definition may include scalar multiplication; the matrix operations of addition, subtraction, and multiplication; or the function INV for the inverse of a matrix. BASIC notation is used for these operations. Legal symbols and functions are listed on the screen. The definition must be made in terms of the names of already defined matrices.

After you enter the definition, it will be displayed again, and you will be asked whether or not you want to use that definition. By typing N for no, you will be given another opportunity to input the definition. A Q will cancel the new definition and take you back to the F1 menu. A Y confirms the new definition and takes you to the next screen, which allows you to write a description for the newly defined matrix.

- Next, you will be asked whether you want to define another dynamic matrix. A Y will take you back through the steps above, and a Q or N will take you back to the F1 menu.

How to Define an Identity or Constant Matrix

- At the F1 menu, type 4 to create an identity or constant matrix. A constant matrix is a matrix in which all entries are the same number. An identity matrix is a matrix with 1s on the diagonal and 0s elsewhere. After entering a 4, you must specify whether you want to create an identity (I) or a constant (C) matrix.

- If you wish to create an identity matrix, you must specify the number of rows. Since this matrix is square, this will automatically be the number of columns. Once you input the number of rows and press Return, you will have the opportunity to give a description of the matrix. Next, the matrix will be displayed, and after pressing Return, you will be asked the name of the matrix. You will then be asked if you would like to define another identity or constant matrix.

- If you wish to create a constant matrix, you must specify the number of rows and columns. Next the software will ask you for the number for the constant matrix. This number will serve as every entry of the matrix. You may then give an optional description, and next the matrix will be displayed. The last step in defining a constant matrix is to give it a name.

How to Edit a Matrix

- To edit a matrix, type 5 at the F1 menu. The message shown for this option states that after modifying a predefined matrix, you will be able to replace the original matrix or save the modified matrix under a different name, so that the original matrix can be retained.

- First you will be asked for the name of the matrix that you wish to edit. (Note that by pressing Return you will bring to the screen an index of all matrices in current memory. Use the arrow keys to highlight the appropriate matrix, and press Return to select that matrix.) Once the name is given and Return is pressed, this predefined matrix will be displayed. Pressing Return will give you the option to Edit an element in matrix. If you do not want this matrix or this option, type Q for quit at this point. An answer of Y for yes and a Return will take you into the upper command window. At this time you will be asked for the row and column of the entry to be edited. Enter this information and press Return; you will be asked for the new entry for the position specified. When you type the new entry and then press Return, you will be shown the edited matrix. Pressing Return again will bring the option Edit an element in matrix back to the screen. This enables you to edit another entry in this matrix. If you type a Y for yes, you will go through the editing process again. Typing N for no will give you the option to replace the matrix. If you decide to replace the matrix (type Y), the edited matrix will replace the predefined one. If you type N, you will be asked for a new name for the edited matrix. If you give no name to the edited matrix and simply hit the Return key at this point, your edited matrix will be discarded and the original will remain. If you provide a name for the edited matrix, then both the edited matrix and the original matrix will be retained in memory.

11 Printing or Viewing a Matrix

Option F2 in the main (F10) menu, Print/View Matrix, gives several ways to look at matrices that have been defined. The actual matrix or the description of the matrix may be viewed on the screen or printed. The F2 menu also allows the user to change the screen display from 40 columns (large print) to 80 columns (small print).

How to View a Matrix

• Type 1 at the F2 menu to view a predefined matrix on the computer screen. The matrix is accessed through its name. No editing can be done within this option; you may only look at the matrix.

• Type 2 to print all or a selection of currently defined matrices. If you decide to print a selection of the matrices, you must select the ones to be printed by their names. (Pressing Return will take you to an index that presents all the names of the matrices that have been defined. Use the arrow keys to highlight the appropriate matrix, and press Return to select that matrix.) When you have completed the list of matrices that you want to print, type a period or decimal (.). Then press Return, and the printing will begin.

• Type 3 to either print or view on screen the name, dimension, description, and type (static or dynamic) of every matrix currently defined. This option will not show the actual entries of the matrix.

How to Change the Display Mode from 40 to 80 Columns

The screens of the *Matrix* software present information in large type. This display is useful for classroom demonstrations. However, when large matrices are used, some columns of the matrix may not appear on the screen. To allow large print for ease in reading as well as the ability to view large matrices on the screen, the software offers the options of 40 columns and 80 columns on the screen display.

• Type 4 at the F2 menu to change the screen display from 40 columns to 80 columns.

(When the software is booted, it will show all output in 40-column mode.) On the screen entitled $\boxed{\text{Change Screen Mode}}$, the current mode will be shown. By selecting F for 40-column mode and E for 80-column mode, you may choose the size of the output on all screens except the menu screens. The menu screens always remain in 40-column mode. Once the mode is changed, it will remain throughout the session unless you come back to this option.

12   The Matrix Calculator

A matrix calculator is located in two menus of the *Matrix* software, F3 and F4. Both matrix calculator options are the same. The calculator allows you to perform scalar multiplication; addition, subtraction, and multiplication of matrices; raising a matrix to a power; and finding the inverse of a matrix. In menu F3, $\boxed{\text{Matrix Calculator}}$, the calculator option is the most important one presented. In menu F4, $\boxed{\text{Matrix Toolkit}}$, the calculator is one of several tools presented for working with matrices.

• To access the matrix calculator, type 1 at the F3 menu or 6 at the F4 menu. Note that you will not be able to define matrices in this option; therefore, you must already have defined the matrices on which you wish to operate. The screen for the Matrix Calculator lists legal symbols of the calculator. You will be asked to write the matrix expression to be calculated using BASIC notation to show operations of multiplication (∗), addition (+), subtraction (−), and power (∧). The matrices are identified by their names. The valid functions that are listed on this screen show numerical functions that can be used in defining scalars for scalar multiplication. For example, a matrix may be multiplied by the scalar log(7).

• Several functions are specific to matrices. The functions INV, TRN, and DET are functions that can have only the name of a matrix as an argument. The function INV finds the inverse of a square matrix. The function TRN finds the transpose of a matrix. The function DET finds the determinant of a square matrix. The function $\text{IDN}(f)$ produces an identity matrix that has f rows and f columns.

• Examples of BASIC notation for various operations are shown in Table 21, where MAT1 and MAT2 are matrices of equal dimension.

Operation	BASIC Notation
Scalar Multiplication	5 ∗ MAT1
Addition	MAT1 + MAT2
Multiplication	MAT1 ∗ MAT2
Inverse of Matrix	INV(MAT1)
Power	(MAT2)∧10

Table 21: BASIC Notation for Matrix Operations

• The software cannot perform operations that are undefined. For example, adding two matrices of different dimension is not defined. An error message will appear if an undefined matrix expression is entered.

• When you access the matrix calculator, you will first be asked for the expression you wish to calculate. Type in this expression using the names of the matrices and BASIC notation. After you press Return, the expression will be printed on the screen with the question Evaluate this expression(Y/N/Q)? . Answering N (no) allows you to input the expression again. Answering Y (yes) will instruct the computer to evaluate the expression and display the result. You will then be given the option to name your result. If the resulting matrix is not named, the matrix will be discarded.

In Section 4.1, the calculations for finding the demand matrix or the production matrix of the Leontief Input-Output Model require a combination of several operations. Once the initial matrices are defined, these calculations can be done with the matrix calculator. For example, using an already defined transition matrix T, an appropriate identity matrix I, and a demand matrix D, you can find the production matrix P by using the matrix calculator to compute the expression

$$INV(I - T) * D$$

and then naming the result P.

• When finding the inverse of a square matrix, the issue of ill-conditioned matrices may arise (see page 27). A function used to judge whether a matrix is ill-conditioned is the *determinant* of a matrix. The determinant is a number that depends on the entries of the matrix. A matrix that has no inverse has a determinant equal to zero. Using the software to find the inverse of a matrix with a determinant of zero will produce the error message "Couldn't take the inverse." If the determinant of a matrix is near zero, then the matrix is ill-conditioned, and a computer-generated inverse may contain significant rounding errors. The software will calculate the inverse of a matrix that has a determinant near zero, but a warning message will be given that includes the value of the determinant.

13   Finding the Inverse of a Matrix

Although the matrix calculator of menus F3 and F4 will compute the inverse of a matrix directly, the inverse can also be found with the *Matrix* software by using Elementary Row Operations (EROs). Menu F4, Matrix Toolkit , contains the options necessary to produce an inverse by using EROs. The procedures accessed in these options serve mainly as tools for learning how to row reduce a matrix, rather than simply for calculating the inverse. Since the software produces entries that are shown as decimals, the inverse produced will have approximate entries.

How to Augment a Matrix

• To find the inverse of a square matrix using EROs, you must first define that matrix and an identity matrix of the same dimension. This is done using menu F1, as described on page 106. The next step is to create an augmented matrix from the matrix you wish to invert and the identity matrix. Type 1 at menu F4 to augment the matrix with the identity matrix. You will first be asked for the left side of the augmented matrix; type the name of the matrix you wish to invert. Next you will be asked for the right side of the augmented matrix. Type the name of the identity matrix. After you press Return, the resulting augmented matrix will be shown on the screen. After another Return, you will be asked to provide a name for this augmented matrix. (Note that if you simply press Return without giving a name, the augmented matrix will be discarded.) You will then be given the opportunity to provide an optional description and asked if you would like to augment another matrix.

How to Row Reduce a Matrix

Once you have defined an augmented matrix, you are ready to perform the appropriate EROs on it.

• At menu F4, type 3 to access the option $\boxed{\text{Row Reduce A Matrix}}$. The software will first ask for the name of the matrix you wish to row reduce. At this time, type the name of the augmented matrix. Your matrix will appear on the screen, and after pressing Return, you will be asked $\boxed{\text{Reduce this matrix(Y/N/Q)?}}$. If you type N for no, you will asked for the name of the matrix again. If you type Y for yes, you will see an important message on the screen: $\boxed{\text{Press D (Done) when you have finished reducing the matrix.}}$ When you have finished row reducing the matrix, you must type D so that the reduced matrix can be saved. Typing Q during the row reduction process will quit the option and discard the results that have been obtained. After pressing Return, you will see the matrix at the top of the screen and a list of three operations, E, M, and R, at the bottom of the screen. These three operations represent the three EROs.

Operation E allows you to exchange rows. If you type E, you will be asked to enter the indexes of the two rows that you want to exchange. Put a space or a comma between the indexes of the two rows. The values of the two row indexes must be integers that represent valid row indexes of the matrix. After pressing Return, you will see the matrix with the two rows exchanged.

Operation M allows you to multiply a row by the reciprocal of a specified entry of the matrix. This operation is useful to transform an entry along the diagonal into a 1. If you type M, you will be asked for the values of I and J, which are the indexes of the row and column of the entry whose reciprocal is to be used. Furthermore, I is the index of the row that will be multiplied by the reciprocal of the entry in row I and column J. In other words, the entry in row I and column J will become a 1 and the other entries in row I will be multiplied by the reciprocal of entry I,J. Integers that represent valid row and column indexes of the matrix must be used for the values of I and J. After you press Return, the matrix will be shown with the operation completed.

Operation R allows you to replace a row with the sum of the row and a multiple of another row. This operation is useful in placing zeros in appropriate entries of the matrix. On typing R, you will be asked for the values of I, J, and K. I is the index of the row whose entries are to be multiplied by the negative of the entry in row J and column K; the products are then added to the entries in row J. The operation will produce a zero entry in row J and column K if the entry in row I and column K is a 1. The other entries in row J also will be changed, but the entries in row I will not be changed. Before using operation R, the entry in row I and column K can be changed to a 1 by using operation M. Values of I and J must represent valid rows of the matrix, and K must represent a valid column of the matrix. After pressing Return, you will see the matrix with the operation completed.

• An option that is not shown in the list on the menu allows you to "undo" the last operation performed. When the list of choices E, M, and R is shown on the bottom of the screen and you are asked to input your choice, you may undo the last operation by pressing the backspace key. (The backspace key normally is used to delete a space to the left of the cursor.) You may undo only the last operation. The process is completed after you press Return, and the screen will show the matrix before the last operation.

• When you have successfully transformed the left side of the augmented matrix into an identity matrix using EROs, the inverse will be the right side of the augmented matrix. At this point you should type D for done. (If you type Q, your work will be lost.) You will then be asked for the name of the resulting matrix. (If you do not give a name, the resulting matrix will be discarded.) You may then give a description, and subsequently you are given the option to row reduce another matrix.

• To obtain the matrix that is the inverse of the original matrix, you will want to extract the right side of the row-reduced augmented matrix. Type 2 at menu F4 to select the option Matrix From Augmented Matrix . You will be asked for the name of the augmented matrix. Once you type the name and press Return, the augmented matrix will be shown. After another Return, you will be asked Use Left or Right side (L/R)? . You can then specify the side of the augmented matrix from which you wish to extract a matrix. If you type L for left, then you will be asked Last column to be used? . Enter the index of the last column to be included in the new matrix. If you type R for right, then you will be asked First column to be used? . Enter the index of the first column to be included in the new matrix. In either response your input must be an integer that refers to a valid column of the augmented matrix. After specifying L or R and pressing Return, the newly formed matrix will be shown. After another Return, the name of the new matrix is requested, and then the opportunity is given to enter a description of this matrix.

How to Perform a Full Pivot

• A semiautomatic method of row reduction called Full Pivot can be accessed by typing 4 in menu F4. Option 4 can be used to row reduce a matrix instead of option 3 described above. Option 4 allows you to row reduce a matrix without specifying all the EROs necessary to place zeros and a single one in a column. When first learning the concepts of EROs, option 3 may be the best choice for a student. Later, perhaps after mastering the use of EROs, option 4 can be used to save some time.

You must first identify the matrix to be reduced. Note that you should type D for done at the end of the process. Once the matrix is displayed, three operations are shown: P for full pivot, E for exchange rows, and D for done.

If you select choice P, you will be asked for the entry about which you wish to pivot. A single pivot encompasses the EROs that transform a specified entry to a 1 and the other entries in that entry's column to zeros. To identify the entry about which to pivot, you must input the row I and column J of that entry. Integers that refer to valid rows and columns of the matrix must be used as values for I and J. Once the pivot is complete, the new matrix will be shown.

If you select choice E, you will be asked for the row indexes M and N of the two rows that will be exchanged. Integers that refer to valid rows of this matrix must be provided for M and N.

The backspace key (see page 113) does not work in this option to undo the last operation.

14   Changing Colors and Timing

The software allows you to change both the colors of the screen displays and the timing of the quits and the opening screen. These options are accessed from the main menu, but they are not listed on the screen display. While at the main menu, press the shift key and 6 key at the same time. This is equivalent to typing ∧ and will display the $\boxed{\text{Program Control Menu}}$ on the screen.

How to Change the Screen Colors

If you are using a projection system that allows only certain colors to be displayed, then some of the graphics and directions may not be visible to the class. To alleviate this problem, the display colors may be changed. To change screen color, you should be in the Program Control Menu.

• Select option 1 of the Program Control Menu to change the color defaults. This selection takes you to the $\boxed{\text{Color Display Control}}$ menu.

• You can change the color of both the text displays and the graphics displays. To change the text displays, type 2 for black and white; type 4 or 5 to choose the colors you wish to use. Text-display changes will alter the colors used in the directions, but not in the graphics.

• To change the colors of the graphics displays, type 6 to access $\boxed{\text{Change Graphics Defaults}}$. This submenu gives you the present graphics defaults (1) or allows you to change the background color (2) and foreground colors (3). Our experience indicates that the foreground colors are generally the cause of not being able to see certain colors on a projection screen.

To change the foreground colors, type 3. You should choose the palette that contains the colors that your projection system will display.

• Once you have changed the color settings, type Q. This returns you to the Color Display Control menu. If you wish to have the new settings become the default settings that are used whenever the software is booted, then type 7. (Be sure that the *Matrix* diskette is in drive A.) If you do not save the present settings, then the original settings will return when the program is booted again.

How to Change the Timing of the Quits and the Opening Screen

The length of display time of the NCSSM logo and the timing of "quick quitting" can be altered by selecting option 2, $\boxed{\text{Change Program Defaults}}$, of the Program Control Menu.

• Quick quitting may be used anytime you type Q to exit an option. After typing Q, you will see $\boxed{\text{Quitting this option}}$ displayed on your screen. If you do nothing, you will return to the previous menu. At this point, however, you can press a function key to go directly to another menu. If you press a function key followed by a number before the screen clears, then you will go directly to an option in another menu.

Options 2 and 3 of the Change Program Defaults menu allow you to change the length of time that you have to make the selections for the next menu, or the next menu and option, once you have typed Q. These changes can be saved using option 5 of this same menu. If you select option 5, the screen display will verify the save. Be sure you have your *Matrix* software disk in drive A when you perform this save.

• The NCSSM logo is presented each time the software is booted. By selecting option 4 of the Change Program Defaults menu, you can change the length of time this logo is displayed. Simply input the number of seconds you wish the logo to remain on the screen and press Return. You will return to the Change Program Defaults menu. Since this option is applicable only to rebooting, you will want to save this change. Option 5 allows you to save the current configuration. Be sure that the *Matrix* diskette is in drive A when you select the save option.

15 Quitting the *Matrix* Program

When you have completed your work with the software, return to the main menu, F10. From this menu type Q. You will be asked if you really want to quit, since perhaps you may have hit Q by mistake. If you do wish to quit the program, type Y and press Return. You will be returned to DOS and the **A>** prompt will appear on the screen.